Nuts in the Kitchen

Also by Susan Herrmann Loomis

Nuts in the Kitchen

More Than 100 Recipes for Every Taste and Occasion

Susan Herrmann Loomis

WILLIAM MORROW

An Imprint of HarperCollins Publishers

HarperCollins books may be purchased for educational, business, or sales promotional use. For information please write: Special Markets Department, HarperCollins Publishers, 10 East 53rd Street, New York, NY 10022.

FIRST EDITION

Designed by Ashley Halsey

Library of Congress Cataloging-in-Publication Data

Loomis, Susan Herrmann.
   Nuts in the Kitchen : more than 100 recipes for every taste and occasion /
Susan Herrmann Loomis.—1st ed.
        p.   cm.
   ISBN 978-0-06-123501-6
   1. Cookery (Nuts)   2. Nuts.   I. Title.
   TX814.L66   2010
   641.6'45—dc22
                                                                 2009044019

10 11 12 13 14   WBC/RRD   10 9 8 7 6 5 4 3 2 1

To Joe and Fiona, my darling children
You continue to amaze me with your graceful acceptance at having to,
for example, eat nut recipes seven nights a week!

Contents

Acknowledgments

It always feels just the slightest bit unfair to claim sole authorship of a book, because so many helpful hands and brains are behind it. So I claim authorship only after thanking those others, often behind the scenes, who made it happen.

There are so many . . . where to begin? With Lena Sodergren, I think. She is my dearest friend and neighbor, and without her friendship and the sheer number of delectable recipes she brought my way, this book wouldn't have come into being. Lena, you're a godsend.

To Patricia Wells, one of few who didn't snicker at nuts and whose conversation and friendship continue to be dear and compelling, even when we're discussing the best way to toast a nut!

To Marion Pruitt, whose gift of hilarity has had me clutching my stomach on more than one occasion as she and I, through the offices of e-mail and telephone, talk recipes and life.

To warm and wonderful James Navé,
whose gift with words has enriched me beyond measure.

To Laura Shapiro, another nonsnickerer and source of inspiration, laughter, great ideas, and general all-around support.

To Harold McGee, friend and colleague, whose response to my endless questions was always rapid and generous.

To my friends Françoise Doré and Alain Juvenon, whose insights and analyses on things in life and art are a constant source of fascination.

To Barbara Leopold, recipe tester and friend, who sticks with me through thick, thin, cakes, soups, and stews, always with elegance.

To Jane Sigal, friend and colleague, emergency recipe tester, and discotheque companion.

To dear Angela Miller, my agent, who encourages, supports, and wastes no words or time in doing so!

To Harriet Bell, editor, friend, lunch

mate—your wicked good humor keeps me laughing, and your editing is a blessing. And to Lyssa, for her ministrations.

To Mary Ellen O'Neill, editor, who swooped in with rapier wit, intelligence, and enthusiasm to gracefully usher this book to production.

To Mac Mackie, assistant editor extraordinaire; to Tavia Kowalchuk, Joanne Minutillo, and Shawn Nicholls for their bright and smart work in making this book known.

As I waded through nutrition information about nuts I became hopelessly muddled and confused by all the claims and counterclaims. I'd been in a similar state as I tried to unravel the nutrition of seafood, and I remembered who'd thrown out the line that pulled me in to the truth. It was Dr. Joyce Nettleton, a nutritionist, food scientist, and author. She has many books to her credit and currently writes a terrific blog called fatsoflife.com. I sent her a plea for help, and she responded, guiding me to the truth about nut nutrition. Joyce is a fine and careful scientist who refuses to walk on thin ice when it comes to nutrition. Here's a glass of vino tinto to you, Joyce!

My trip to east Anatolia wouldn't have been possible without the help of Sara Baer-Sinnott of Oldways Preservation and Trust. Through Sara's help came one of the angels of this book, Filiz Hosukuglo, cooking consultant and writer from Gaziantep, Turkey. Filiz was my "open sesame" to everything about nuts, Anatolian cuisine, and a host of great adventures in and around Gaziantep. I also thank dear Paula Wolfert, friend and colleague, whose constant generosity and encouragement remain undiminished. Thank you, too, to Necmettin Kaymaz, Dr. Kamil Sarpkaya, to Mustafa Ozguler for his *katmer* and *loukoum,* and last but far from least, to the Singing Syrians, dear Temim Kasmo, Hamza Hamza, and Mahmoud Zein Alabidin.

My trip to Thailand was magical, thanks to Andrew Ricker, who was the sole instrument of its creation. I owe him greatly for his depth of knowledge and friendly generosity, for he even went so far as to climb on the head of an elephant with me, something he'd said he would never do. Thank you, too, to Sunny Bowornat and Sunneemas Noree, food and cooking friends and colleagues.

Others I want to thank for their generosity, help, and friendship include Johan Sodergren in Sweden, Kerrie Luzum in Italy, Manuela Devisme in southern Spain, my sweet Eloise Perret in France, Carolyn Johnson in France, Karen Coates in New Mexico and Asia, Anne Leblanc and the entire Leblanc family in France, Doris and Joe Herrmann—Mother and Dad—in Portland, Oregon.

Without my friends in Louviers, working on this book would have been a dry and lonely pursuit, for they tasted, they laughed, they comforted, they encouraged. I salute you, Betty Phillipe and Louis Garcia, Babette and Jean-Lou Dawaele, Edith and Bernard Leroy, Michel and Chantal Amsalem, Christian and Nadine Devisme, Hervé Lestage, everyone in my wine tasting group, particularly Fred Heldt, Marie Boivin, Patricia and Baptiste Bourdon. Thank you to everyone at Clet Epicerie Fine, particularly Isabelle, to Mr. Dragonelli at Boucherie des Saisons, to everyone at Pâtisserie Nicolas Gosselin.

Thank you to my friend Lisa Higgins at *Metropolitan Home* magazine, for her loyalty, to Karen Taylor, editor of *France* magazine, Judy Fayard, editor of *France Today*, and Mary Margaret Chappell, food editor for *Vegetarian Times*.

A big thank-you to Mr. Frederic Rosengarten, Jr., whom I have not met but whose wonderful book *The Book of Edible Nuts* is a work of true passion and scholarship.

Introduction

Nuts. They're salty, buttery, crunchy, toasty, and simply delicious. For many, they're one of those fatty, guilty pleasures reserved for rare occasions. As an ingredient they aren't taken the least bit seriously, or so I realized when I responded to the question of what project I was currently working on. All I had to say was "A book about nuts" and laughter and snickers followed. For all of you comedians out there, should you ever need material, look to nuts for the answer. The entire subject is a potential gold mine.

The nut joke is limited mostly to North America, where nuts show up at baseball games or in big bowls in front of the TV. Travel to countries in the Middle East, Asia, Africa, and Europe, whose cuisines naturally incorporate or even depend on the nut, and you'll encounter an entirely different situation. No jokes, no guilt—just pure and unadulterated pleasure in the eating. And that is the reason for this book.

It's time. We endlessly search for new flavor and texture experiences, and nuts satisfy. And just as important, current scientific and medical research is showing nutritional benefits that are hard to ignore. The role of nuts in the North American and European vegan diet is vital, for they offer a delectable source of protein, minerals, and other nutrients; they provide umami, or the savory sensation that also comes from meat; and they thicken in a similar way to flour and butter.

I'm all for laughing—after all, laughter is the best medicine. And snickers don't bother me in the least. In fact, I occasionally feel as though I've had the last laugh. Why wouldn't I? In the course of working on this book I traveled to and gained insight into fascinating and unfamiliar cultures. I spent time with great people, tasted amazing dishes and learned how to make most of them, and got to write about it all. And finally, but not finally at all, I get to treat myself, my family, my friends, and you to scrumptiously flavorful dishes.

You will read some of the current

nutritional claims about nuts. They appear to be little medical miracles. While this is exciting, even more fulfilling is that they're culinary miracles as well. When ground and added to a sauce or soup, they act as a thickener; they make a terrific flour replacement, particularly in cakes and coatings. And their range of toasty flavors enhances everything from seafood to meat.

If cultures that regularly incorporate nuts into their cuisines are used as models, nuts can be served at any point in the meal. In Syria, for example, a mixture of toasted nuts and seeds similar to Dukkah (page 50) is part of breakfast, along with olive oil, yogurt, bread, and vegetables.

In Europe, nuts are used with abandon in sweets and are also tossed into many a savory dish. The same is true in northern Africa and in Asia. Adding ground almonds to a soup to thicken it and turn it into a rich, subtle cream, for example, is a secret from the Spanish countryside. In Italy, local pine nuts blend into pesto, but in these pages the heady crispness of Brazil nuts teams with parsley and basil to give the fresh sauce its zest. Walnuts are normally highly esteemed for the buttery crunch they add to baked goods. Here they play that role with millet and herbs, saffron and cilantro, to make a haunting, richly flavored salad. Pistachios add luxury to a melting chocolate tart, along with their vivid color and sweet crunch.

Finding the recipes in this book has been a whirlwind of a lovely time. I knew I could write a wonderful book with exclusively French recipes, but I didn't want this book to be so France-centric, so I traveled to learn, eat, and steal (recipes and techniques, that is!). Stories of my travels were met with nearly as much mirth (and incredulity) as the subject of this book. No one could believe I went all the way to Thailand to research nuts, but why wouldn't I go to a country where peanuts figure in nearly every recipe and rural families almost all have a peanut plot to call their own? Traveling to Sweden had that goal as well (the Manu Chao concert was fun too), and Turkey was a must, for I had to get to the bottom of the fabled pistachio. And there, in the Fertile Crescent, I not only found what I was looking for, but the poet in me found its home. Who wouldn't melt at the idea of pistachio music (see page 70) and all the other poetry in that marvelous land?

Nuts in Italian and Spanish cuisines are familiar to most of us, but I checked back into both countries to reaffirm things. And then there is the use of nuts in Eastern Europe and beyond. Suffice it to say that most cultures value nuts for the pleasurable flavors and textures they offer to everything from soup to dessert—their nutritive value is simply a plus. And this book is oriented the same way. You can learn here about how healthful nuts are, and I hope you will read the carefully prepared section on nutrition and nuts. But mostly you can savor the delicious aspects of nuts, what makes them more than simply a snack food.

I wish you good times and good cooking with this book about nuts. Enjoy it all, use it well, and *bon appétit*!

Nuts and Seeds: Why They're So Good for Us

When it comes to nuts and seeds, the health claims don't end. Nuts are touted as the solution to everything from cardiac and bone health to weight loss and joint flexibility. What becomes evident on closer inspection into all these claims is that all may be true, but much has yet to be established.

What is beyond a doubt, however, is that nuts are highly nutritious. Consider the following discoveries: The fats contained in them are "good" and are thought to do for the body what WD-40 does for a machine—ease the passage, loosen the joints. The studies suggest that nuts are anti-inflammatory. Should this prove an ironclad medical and scientific conclusion, the implications are stunning, for inflammation is most likely at the root of many of our "modern" afflictions. Thus regular, moderate consumption of nuts could reduce the occurrence and development of many ills.

But wait! There's more! Nuts are cholesterol-free and proven to diminish the risk of heart disease. They contain a variety of minerals and a dense amount of protein, which makes them satisfying powerhouses of energy. And surprisingly enough, those who incorporate nuts regularly into their diet don't gain weight.

This doesn't mean that we should suddenly begin popping open cans of fried and salted nuts and wolfing them down. Instead, it means a handful of nuts each day may keep the doctor at bay.

Many dramatic health claims are made about the oils in nuts and seeds. They contain healthful, unsaturated fatty acids, primarily monounsaturated fats, the kind that stay liquid at room temperature and solidify when chilled (a useful image to show their liquid state in the body) and can help reduce bad cholesterol in the blood, which contributes to a lower risk of heart disease and stroke.

What is most vital about nuts and seeds is the rich flavor and texture they can add to everything from breakfast cereal to braised chicken. They are ideal for moments of extreme hunger and after vigorous exercise, for their high energy content makes you feel full for much longer than most foods, making a little go a long way.

I've compiled a list of the most popular nuts and seeds with some brief information about their major nutrient content and potential health benefits. Read this material over; it is interesting to know some of the nutritional specifics about nuts, and the advice contained here is good information. Then forget what you've read and retain the following: Nuts are healthful when eaten in moderation.

For the real information, turn to the recipes. Once you've recognized the general goodness of nuts, all you need to do is eat and enjoy them.

All of the nutritional information in this section has been reviewed for accuracy by Dr. Joyce A. Nettleton, D.Sc., an internationally recognized nutritional expert.

What Is a Handful?

I mention eating a "handful" of nuts, but what is a handful? Well, a handful has been quantified by various nut boards, nutritionists, and nut commissions, and what it boils down to is the following: when it come to almonds, hazelnuts, and other small varieties, the accepted number hovers around twenty-five individual nuts. For walnuts, it is about eight whole nuts, and the same goes for macadamias; for Brazil nuts, a handful is absolutely no more than six (that fills a *big* hand), as more can be unhealthful.

What Is Raw?

What is a raw nut? Untoasted, unsalted, the way nature made it. Raw nuts are pure and intact, but fear not, for toasting a nut, which substantially increases its flavor, has little impact on its nutritional worth. As for salt, in most cases, a little never hurt.

Nuts

A fact to keep in mind in this section: fat in nuts is the healthy kind.

Almonds: Within the slightly wrinkled brown skin of an almond is a storehouse of energy.

Almonds are among the plant world's richest sources of vitamin E, an antioxidant (any substance that reduces damage due to oxygen) that can contribute to heart and cell health. The skin of the almond contains something called a *flavonoid*, which teams up with its vitamin E to more than double the antioxidant properties of the almond and thus its ability to help the heart and other organs. Almonds supply manganese (which helps to maintain bones and normal blood sugar levels), copper (which among other things plays a role in the flexibility of blood vessels, bones, and joints and in iron utilization), and protein (vital for muscle mass and tissue repair, among other things).

Almonds are 21 percent protein and 49 percent fat. Of that, 30 percent is monounsaturated fat and 12 percent is polyunsaturated fat, both of which are "healthy fats."

Brazil Nuts: These provide the richest source of selenium in the food supply. Selenium may contribute to the prevention of prostate and other cancers, as well as heart disease, and it counteracts the potential toxicity of mercury. However, the U.S. Institute of Medicine recommends not eating more than six Brazil nuts a day to avoid potential selenium toxicity.

Brazil nuts are 14 percent protein and 66 percent fat. Of that, 24 percent is monounsaturated fat and 21 percent is polyunsaturated fat.

Cashews: Cashews are somewhat lower in fat than other nuts, which helps them stay fresh longer. About half their fat is unsaturated. Of this, about 70 percent is oleic acid, which is the same heart-healthy fat found in olive oil. Cashews also contain manganese (see almonds).

Cashews are 18 percent protein and 44 percent fat. Of that, 24 percent is monounsaturated and 8 percent polyunsaturated.

Hazelnuts: Also called *filberts* or *cobnuts*, hazelnuts contain some folate (or vitamin B_9), which helps the body make new protein and red blood cells, helps to produce DNA, and may help reduce cancer, depression, and the risk of neural tube birth defects. Hazelnuts also contain generous amounts of copper and manganese.

Hazelnuts are 15 percent protein and 61 percent fat. Of that, 46 percent is monounsaturated and 8 percent polyunsaturated.

Macadamias: High in monounsaturated fat (they are nearly 60 percent monounsaturated fat), they provide a generous amount of manganese, which helps in the production of insulin, is necessary to activate vitamin C, helps to neutralize poisons in the blood, and helps keep cellular membranes healthy. They also offer a quarter of the daily requirement for thiamine (vitamin B_1).

Macadamias are 8 percent protein and 76 percent fat. Of that, 59 percent is monounsaturated, while 1 percent is polyunsaturated.

Peanuts: Peanuts are an honorary nut, because technically they are legumes growing underground rather than on a tree. They contain the most protein of any member of the nut family. Peanuts contain a plentiful amount of niacin. (Niacin, or vitamin B_3, assists in the functioning of the digestive system, skin, and nerves and is important for the conversion of food to energy.) A 1-ounce portion of peanuts will provide about one-fifth of the daily requirement of niacin.

Peanuts contain folate (see hazelnuts) and resveratrol, a compound that is also found in several grape varieties, including those that go into the making of red wine, and that has been associated with reduced cardiovascular disease and reduced cancer risk.

Aflatoxin is a term associated with peanuts that merits explanation. Aflatoxin is a highly carcinogenic toxin produced by mold that can form in certain foods, including peanuts. To prevent the formation of aflatoxin in peanuts, a biological pesticide is used to treat the soil around the crop. To further protect against aflatoxin, the USDA and the EU (European Union) require stringent testing of peanuts before they are put on the market.

Peanuts are 25 percent protein and 48 percent fat. Of that, 25 percent is monounsaturated fat and 15 percent is polyunsaturated fat.

Pecans: Pecans are unique because they contain fluoride—just 1 ounce will provide 70 percent of the recommended daily amount. They have less protein than most other nuts and are high in monounsaturated fat, making them similar to macadamias. Pecans are high in manganese and copper (see almonds and hazelnuts). Pecans are 9 percent protein and 72 percent fat. Of that, 41 percent is monounsaturated and 22 percent is polyunsaturated.

Pine Nuts: Like walnuts, pine nuts contain more polyunsaturated than monounsaturated fats.

They contain 14 percent protein and 68 percent fat. Of that, 19 percent is monounsaturated and 34 percent polyunsaturated.

Pistachios: Pistachios contain carotenoids, which have been associated with a reduced risk of macular degeneration, an eye disease that may develop later in life. They are higher in fiber than most nuts. Pistachios are most commonly sold salted, and the salt may present problems for those with high blood pressure. Pistachios are 21 percent protein and 44 percent fat. Of that, 23 percent is monounsaturated and 13 percent polyunsaturated.

Walnuts: Walnuts contain the short-chain omega-3 alpha-linolenic acid, the only omega-3 found in plants. The short-chain omega-3s may not be as good for the heart as their long-chain cousins (which are found mostly in fish and shellfish), but they are helpful to the heart and helpful in improving the balance of polyunsaturated fatty acids in the diet. Walnuts are also the most abundant food source of copper and manganese.

Walnuts contain 15 percent protein and 65 percent fat. Of that, 9 percent is monounsaturated and 47 percent polyunsaturated.

Seeds

Like nuts, seeds may lower cholesterol in the body because of their unsaturated fatty acids. They offer many of the same nutritional benefits of nuts and much flavor and texture as well.

Flax Seeds: These are a very rich source of the same short-chain omega-3 fatty acid found in walnuts. In addition, flax seeds are concentrated in lignan, which is an excellent source of dietary fiber. For the benefits of flax seeds to be made available to the body, they must be ground or crushed into a meal.

Flax seeds are 18 percent protein and 42 percent fat. Of that, 8 percent is monounsaturated and 29 percent polyunsaturated.

Poppy Seeds: The fat in poppy seeds is rich in heart-healthy short-chain omega-3 and omega-6 fatty acids. Note: Eating poppy seeds—even the amount on a poppy seed bagel—can interfere with a standard drug test for up to ten days after consumption, making the test show a positive reaction to drug use.

Poppy seeds are 18 percent protein and 45 percent fat. Of that, 6 percent is monounsaturated and 31 percent is polyunsaturated.

Pumpkin Seeds: These are exceptional in the plant world because they provide iron (1 ounce supplies up to 23 percent of a woman's daily requirement) and zinc, which is important to immune and neurological function, may promote prostate and bone health in men, helps in wound healing and maintenance of the sense of taste and smell, and is needed for DNA synthesis. Pumpkin seeds are also a good source of magnesium, manganese, phosphorus, copper, and vitamin K, which is necessary for normal blood clotting.

Pumpkin seeds are 24 percent protein and 45 percent fat. Of that, 14 percent is monounsaturated fat and 21 percent is polyunsaturated fat.

Sesame Seeds: Sesame seeds and their ground version, tahini or sesame butter, contain iron, copper, manganese, and zinc.

Sesame seeds are 17 percent protein and 50 percent fat. Of that, 19 percent is monounsaturated and 22 percent is polyunsaturated

Sunflower Seeds: Sunflower seeds are an excellent source of vitamins B and E (1 cup of seeds in the shell provides the daily requirement of both), copper (see almonds for both), magnesium, and selenium (see Brazil nuts for

both). Sunflower seeds are also a good source of protein, and half of their fat content is linoleic acid (omega-6—which is essential for growth and development), and half is monounsaturated. They contain substantial amounts of potassium (which can contribute to lowering blood pressure), thiamine (vitamin B_1, which helps the body cells convert carbohydrates into energy and is essential for the functioning of the heart, muscles, and nervous system), riboflavin (vitamin B_2, which works with other B vitamins, helps in cell production, and helps release energy from carbohydrates), and folate (see hazelnuts).

Sunflower seeds contain 21 percent protein and 51 percent fat. Of that, 18 percent is monounsaturated and 23 percent is polyunsaturated.

Nut Allergies

The proteins in certain nuts, primarily peanuts but other nuts as well, can provoke mild to severe allergic reactions. The most severe reaction is called *anaphylaxis*, which is a sudden, severe, whole-body reaction that can range from mild to fatal. If testing for allergies reveals an allergy to nuts, the only way to avoid an allergic reaction is to completely avoid nuts; all foods containing nuts; foods, surfaces, dishes, and utensils that have been in contact with nuts; and even nut particles in the air, if in an enclosed space where people are cracking and eating nuts.

Nuts in the Kitchen

Breakfast

Apricot and Pine Nut Compote

Crunchy Granola

Heavenly Chocolate Hazlenut Spread

Apricot Pistachio Compote

Almond Cake

Nutty Pancakes

Orange and Almond Pashka

Fruit Crisp with Almond Topping

Quinoa, Hazelnut, and Cornmeal Pancakes

Waffles with Walnut Whipped Cream

Breakfast

Breakfast may be the most important meal of the day, for the nutritional foundation it provides. It's my favorite meal as well, because breakfast foods are so great—a stack of nutty pancakes drizzled with maple syrup, crisp granola filled with nuts and dried fruits, fresh fruit compotes, yogurt parfaits, cakes and waffles, a lush almond cake.

I've included some of my favorite breakfast foods here, and most of them are sweet. I also love to sprinkle Dukkah (page 50) on a piece of toast that I've moistened with olive oil; the Almond Sprinkle (page 234) is delicious over yogurt; and sometimes nothing hits the spot like almond butter (page 224) spread on a piece of freshly baked bread.

Breakfast is new, it's fresh, it's light and luscious. Accompany these dishes with coffee or tea, almond milk, or freshly squeezed juice. You'll feel like a million bucks all day long.

Apricot and Pine Nut Compote

❋ Makes 6 to 8 servings

I was staying with my friend Patricia Wells, and she served a gorgeous compote like this, made with apricots straight from her own trees. I swooned—then ate some more!

Note: *The recipe calls for lavender honey, which is best, but if you cannot find it, use a floral honey that is on the mild side. The amount of honey you use really depends on your sweet tooth and the sweet ripeness of the apricots.*

2 pounds (1 kg) fresh apricots, halved, peeled, and pitted

3 tablespoons lavender honey

3 tablespoons pine nuts

1. Place the apricots in a large, heavy saucepan over medium heat. They will first sizzle and then give up their juices. Cook until they are tender and very juicy, about 20 minutes, then stir in the honey and continue cooking for an additional 10 minutes. Remove the compote from the stove, stir in the pine nuts, and either serve immediately or let cool to room temperature first.

Crunchy Granola

This crunchy mixture of grains and seeds is so beguiling it's hard not to eat it by the handful. Which, actually, isn't the worst way to eat this nutritious and delicious breakfast cereal. Consider it as a snack. If you're not a milk drinker, try pouring fresh apple juice over this instead, with a topping of yogurt. Serve it with fresh fruit, use it as a topping for hot cereal, or stir it into muffins or sweet breads. It's versatile and delicious.

1 cup (16 tablespoons; 250 g) unsalted butter

¼ cup (60 ml) mild honey

¼ cup (55 g) dark brown sugar

¼ teaspoon sea salt

1 teaspoon vanilla extract

4 cups rolled oats or flakes made from other grains

1 cup (90 g) unsweetened coconut

¼ cup (40 g) sunflower seeds

⅓ cup (35 g) sesame seeds

⅓ cup (30 g) raw almonds

Note: *Use this recipe as a guide. You may add other seeds or nuts, other grains like buckwheat or quinoa flakes or even chickpea flakes (don't use rice flakes, though; they're tough). Use more or less honey or brown sugar, or all honey or all brown sugar, but know that if you use all honey the granola is likely to brown much more quickly. In fact, even with the amount of honey called for, the granola tends to brown quickly, so don't leave the kitchen as it is baking. And don't leave out the vanilla!*

Unsweetened coconut is available at health food and specialty stores.

1. Preheat the oven to 350°F (180°C). Line a baking sheet with parchment paper or aluminum foil.

2. Place the butter in a medium saucepan over medium heat. When it has melted enough to cover the bottom of the pan, add the honey and brown sugar and whisk occasionally as the butter melts. When it is fully melted, gently whisk in the salt and vanilla. Remove from the heat.

3. Place the grains, coconut, seeds, and almonds in a large bowl. Pour the sauce—it may still be very hot, which is fine—over the mixture. Toss until all the ingredients are thoroughly combined, then turn out the granola onto two baking sheets. Spread it out into an even layer and bake in the center of the oven, stirring occasionally, until the granola is golden, 20 to 25 minutes. (Remember that if you've used exclusively honey you should reduce the baking time. Watch it—you'll know when the granola is ready by its golden color.)

4. Remove from the heat and let cool, then break up the clumps and transfer to airtight containers and store in a cool spot. The granola will keep well for about 1 month.

Heavenly Chocolate Hazelnut Spread

🍀 *Makes about 2 cups (500 ml)*

The title says it all, and, yes, I was inspired by Nutella to make this luscious spread. I adore Nutella, and this is even better, more richly flavored, more elegant. And it makes a relatively small quantity, so it is something to truly savor, every single mouthful.

Nutella is that sinfully rich chocolate and hazelnut spread that Mr. Pietro Ferrero, an Italian candy magnate from Piemonte, Italy, developed after World War II. Chocolate was in short supply and taxes on it were high, so to extend it Mr. Ferrero ground the sweet, local *tonde gentile* hazelnut to a paste and added it to chocolate. He had a model to follow, for *giandujotti,* small hazelnut and chocolate confections developed to cut back on the costs of pure chocolate confections in the mid-1800s, had already made Turin candy makers famous throughout Italy.

Mr. Ferrero's chocolate-extender took the form of a Velveeta-like block, ready for slicing and slapping between two pieces of bread. It wasn't until several years later that Mr. Ferrero turned his mixture into one of spreadable consistency. Sometime later he and his colleagues renamed it Nutella. Today its popularity knows no bounds, and it is available in everything from tiny tablespoon-sized containers to giant 2-pound jars.

2 cups (300 g) hazelnuts

¾ cup (90 g) confectioners' sugar

¼ cup (40 g) good-quality unsweetened dark cocoa powder, such as Valrhona or Scharffen Berger

Pinch of salt

2 tablespoons canola oil, or more if necessary (optional)

Note: *This spread is as addictive as its inspiration. I add 5 tablespoons of cocoa to the mixture, which gives it a very satisfying chocolate and hazelnut flavor— you may want to add a bit more or a bit less.*

I call for neutral oil here, which gives it a lovely spreadable consistency. If you leave out the oil— which I do on occasion—the flavor is still the same, but it is a bit more solid and less easy to spread.

Finally, don't expect the completely smooth texture of commercial Nutella here. Think of this as the "crunchy" version!

1. Preheat the oven to 375°F (190°C). Spread the hazelnuts on a jelly-roll pan and toast them until you can smell them, about 10 minutes. Remove them from the oven and place them in a cotton towel. Scrub and roll them around in the towel to remove the skins.

2. When the hazelnuts are skinned (don't be concerned if you cannot remove all the skin—just do the best you can), place the hazelnuts in a food processor and process until the nuts make a smooth paste, which will take some time, about 10 minutes. Add the confectioners' sugar and cocoa powder and process again until all the ingredients are thoroughly mixed. Add the salt, process, and if the mixture is very dry, add the canola oil while the machine is running. Taste for seasoning. If the mixture is very warm, let it cool completely before transferring it to a jar and sealing it. It will keep for about 1 month in a cool, dark spot.

Apricot Pistachio Compote

🌿 *Makes 6 to 8 servings*

What better way to start the day than with a bowl of fresh apricot compote studded with pistachio nuts? I like to serve this freshly made and warm or layered with yogurt in a parfait.

2 pounds (1 kg) apricots, pitted and cut into quarters

2/3 cup (140 g) muscovado or dark brown sugar, lightly packed

Seeds from 4 cardamom pods, crushed (about ¼ teaspoon)

Zest of ½ lemon, minced

2 teaspoons unsalted butter

¼ cup (30 g) pistachio nuts

Pinch of salt

Note: *The amount of sugar you use will depend on your sweet tooth and the sweet ripeness of the apricots.*

I love this hot from the stove, but you can also make it the night before and serve it either chilled or at room temperature.

1. Place the apricots and ½ cup (112 g) of the sugar in a nonreactive saucepan and let sit until the apricots soften and begin to give up their liquid, at least 1 hour. Place the saucepan over medium heat, stir the apricots and sugar and the liquid the apricots have given up, and bring the mixture to a gentle boil. Cook, stirring frequently to keep the compote from sticking to the bottom of the pan, for 30 minutes.

2. Add the cardamom and lemon zest and continue cooking, stirring frequently, until the apricots have turned from a bright orange color to a darkened, rusty color and the juices have thickened somewhat, 30 minutes. Remove from the heat and let cool to lukewarm before serving.

3. Melt the butter in a small skillet over medium heat and add the pistachios. Cook, stirring constantly, until the pistachios are golden on the outside, 5 to 8 minutes. Sprinkle with the salt, stir, and remove from the heat.

4. When the compote is cool enough to serve, divide it evenly among six to eight dishes. Sprinkle each dish with a teaspoon of the remaining brown sugar and an equal amount of pistachios. Serve.

Almond Cake

🍀 *Makes 6 to 8 servings*

Moist, not too sweet, just slightly exotic with the almonds and the orange flower water, this makes a perfect breakfast treat, though it is actually a traditional North African dessert. Cut it into diamond shapes and serve it accompanied by dried and fresh fruits and a steaming bowl of lightly sweetened mint tea or coffee.

2 cups (300 g) almond flour

2½ cups (200 g) fresh bread crumbs

2 teaspoons fine sea salt

1 teaspoon baking powder

¼ teaspoon ground cinnamon

8 large eggs

Seeds from 2 vanilla beans

¾ cup (150 g) vanilla sugar

2 teaspoons orange flower water

3 tablespoons (45 g) unsalted butter, melted and cooled

Note: *To remove the seeds from a vanilla bean, slit it down its length and, using a small spoon, scrape the moist black seeds from the interior of the bean. Save the bean for another use.*

If you cannot find almond flour (though it is readily available at grocery stores and at bobsredmill.com), simply grind almonds in a food processor with a pinch of sugar, until they are a fine powder.

To make vanilla sugar, put 8 cups sugar in an airtight container with 2 vanilla beans and let it sit for 1 week. You may continue to use the same vanilla beans for up to 4 months.

1. Preheat the oven to 400°F (200°C). Butter a 9-inch square (22.5-cm square) cake pan.

2. In a medium bowl, thoroughly mix together the almond flour, bread crumbs, salt, baking powder, and cinnamon.

3. Place the eggs in a large bowl or the bowl of an electric mixer and whisk until they are thoroughly broken up. They don't need to be foamy or thick. Add the vanilla seeds and sugar and whisk until thoroughly combined.

4. Stir the dry ingredients into the egg mixture and mix just until all are combined. Fold in the orange flower water and melted butter, then pour the mixture into the prepared cake pan and bake until golden and firm, 25 to 30 minutes.

5. Remove the cake from the oven and place it on a cooling rack. When the cake has cooled slightly, cut it into 1½-inch (4-cm) diamonds, let it cool entirely, then serve.

Nutty Pancakes

❧ *Makes 4 to 6 servings*

There is nothing quite like an early autumn or winter morning in Louviers, when the dark of night enshrouds our chilly house. The coal stove in the kitchen emits a halo of warmth, a fire burns in the fireplace if the temperature is really low, and I often decide to make pancakes. I've developed many recipes over the years, and this is my current favorite because it combines everything I love—ground almonds for texture and nutrition, a touch of sugar for fun and flavor, a bit of spelt flour for texture and ease, vanilla to make it smooth. Try this recipe, which goes together in a thrice, and you'll see what I mean!

2 cups (500 ml) milk

2 tablespoons (30 g) unsalted butter

1¾ cups (245 g) unbleached all-purpose flour

½ cup spelt flour

1 teaspoon fine sea salt, plus a pinch

2 teaspoons baking powder

½ cup (75 g) raw almonds, finely ground

2 large eggs, separated if desired

1 teaspoon vanilla extract

2 tablespoons vanilla sugar (page 10)

Note: *I always first clean the bowl for whisking egg whites with white vinegar because any oil or crumb will prevent the egg whites from increasing in volume. If the early morning hour has you wanting simply to get from one end of the recipe to the other without the added complication of whisking, omit that step. Whisking gives extra lightness, but it's not required.*

Don't overlook leftover pancakes—spread one with a light layer of butter, sprinkle it with cinnamon sugar, top it with another pancake, and you've got a great after-school treat.

1. Place the milk and butter in a medium saucepan over low heat and heat the milk just until the butter is melted. Remove from the heat to cool to lukewarm.

2. Sift the flours, 1 teaspoon salt, and the baking powder into a large mixing bowl. Add the almonds and mix them into the other dry ingredients using your fingers or a wooden spoon.

3. Whisk the egg yolks, vanilla extract, and sugar into the cooled milk mixture until they are thoroughly combined. Slowly whisk the milk mixture into the dry ingredients, whisking just until all the ingredients are combined.

4. Whisk the egg whites with a pinch of salt in a clean bowl until they make soft peaks, then fold them into the batter.

5. Place a large nonstick skillet over medium heat. When the skillet is hot, pour the batter by ¼-cup amounts into the ungreased hot pan, leaving about ½ inch between pancakes. When the pancakes have bubbled on top, the bubbles have popped, and the undersides of the pancakes are golden, flip the pancakes and cook them until the other side is golden and cooked, which will take just a moment or two. It is hard to give a time for this, as it depends so much on the heat, the thickness of the pan, and the temperature of the batter, but allow for the whole process to take about 5 minutes. Continue with the remaining batter. Serve the pancakes hot from the griddle.

Orange and Almond Pashka

❧ *Makes about 18 servings*

Every Easter for twenty-five years I've made pashka, tweaking it, modifying it, improving it. No matter the version, it is always the favorite dish on a table laden with delicacies. This is my favorite rendition, for its creamy texture is laced with orange and vanilla, slightly crunchy with almonds. I always serve freshly baked kugelhopf with pashka—a sublime combination. Any good, fresh, slightly sweet bread is perfect for spreading with pashka, though it is also delicious on its own.

I serve pashka as a breakfast/brunch dish and occasionally serve it as a dessert too.

3 pounds (1.5 kg) whole-milk yogurt

1 pound (450 g) unsalted butter, at room temperature

2 cups (400 g) vanilla sugar (page 10)

3 large egg yolks

Zest of 1 large orange, preferably organic, minced

5 ounces (140 g) almonds, lightly toasted and coarsely chopped

8 ounces (250 g) dried apricots, preferably unsulfured

Edible flowers for optional garnish

Note: *You may substitute any high-quality dried fruits for the apricots. I recommend unsulfured fruits, which haven't been treated to retain their color.*

Molding the pashka in a flowerpot is traditional, but you can use any shape of mold you like.

I like to garnish pashka with spring flowers—pansies, tiny little daisies, even dandelion petals.

1. Line a fine-mesh sieve with two layers of cheesecloth and place the sieve over a large bowl. Line a very clean 8-cup (2-liter) terra-cotta flowerpot or other mold that has drainage holes with two layers of cheesecloth, leaving the edges of the cheesecloth hanging over the sides of the mold.

2. Place the yogurt in the lined sieve and set over a large bowl. Let the yogurt drain, refrigerated, overnight, or for at least 8 hours. Discard the liquid, reserving the yogurt.

3. In a large bowl or the bowl of an electric mixer, whisk the butter until it is soft and pale yellow. Whisk in the sugar until the mixture is light and pale yellow. Gradually whisk in the drained yogurt and continue whisking until it is thoroughly incorporated and the mixture is smooth and creamy. Whisk in the egg yolks and orange zest until combined thoroughly. Then, using a spatula or wooden spoon, fold in the almonds and the dried apricots so they are evenly dispersed throughout the mixture.

4. Turn the pashka into the prepared mold, then fold the edges of the cheesecloth over the mixture. Set the mold in a shallow dish. Place a plate that is just slightly smaller than the circumference of the mold atop the mold and weight it with a 2-pound (1-kg) can of fruit or vegetables or any 2-pound (1-kg) weight. Refrigerate for at least 24 hours.

5. To serve the pashka, remove it from the shallow dish, discarding any liquid that has drained from it. Remove the weight and plate and place an attractive serving dish or platter over the mold. Flip the mold so the pashka falls gently onto the serving dish. Remove the cheesecloth and garnish with the flowers, if desired. Serve chilled.

Fruit Crisp with Almond Topping

🍀 *Makes 4 to 6 servings*

Call this a crisp or a crumble, it ranks way high on the list of favorite desserts in France. Yes, an import from England, the crisp and the crumble (both called crumble or crumbeuhl) are on the menu at restaurants, offered in patisseries, and served in homes throughout the land.

This almondy crisp/crumble is a favorite for breakfast at my house. I often serve it with crème fraîche or Greek yogurt alongside. The addition of fresh rosemary adds an incomparable flavor.

2½ pounds (1.25 kg) fruit (pears, apples, apricots, rhubarb, etc.), cored or pitted as needed and thinly sliced

⅓ cup (60 g) vanilla sugar (page 10)

2 tablespoons fresh rosemary leaves

⅓ cup (75 g) dark brown sugar, gently packed

½ cup (70 g) unbleached all-purpose flour

8 tablespoons (1 stick/110 g) unsalted butter, cut into small pieces, chilled

1 cup rolled oats

FOR THE TOPPING:

½ cup (70 g) sliced almonds

1 tablespoon vanilla sugar (page 10)

Note: *If you make this the night before, warm it up for 10 minutes before you plan to serve it.*

The crisp is best with mixed fruits, such as apples and pears, peaches and apricots, or nectarines and plums.

There is a relatively small amount of sugar in this recipe because good, ripe fruit has so much of its own. However, you may want to pass a bowl of sugar alongside, for those who desire more.

1. Preheat the oven to 350°F (180°C). Butter an 11 × 9-inch (28 × 23-cm) baking dish.

2. In a large bowl, toss the fruit with the ⅓ cup (60 g) vanilla sugar. Coarsely chop the rosemary and mix it in, then turn the fruit mixture into the prepared baking dish.

3. In a food processor, process the brown sugar with the flour until mixed. Add the butter and pulse until the mixture resembles coarse cornmeal. Turn the mixture into a bowl and add the oats, either by stirring with a wooden spoon or by massaging the oats into the mixture with your hands. Spoon the mixture over the fruit, making an even layer. Sprinkle the almonds on top and sprinkle them with the tablespoon of vanilla sugar.

4. Bake until the fruit is tender and the topping is crisp and golden, about 1 hour. Serve warm.

Quinoa, Hazelnut, and Cornmeal Pancakes

🍀 *Makes 4 to 6 servings*

These cakes offer a symphony of crunch, from the quinoa, the cornmeal, and the hazelnuts. They are substantial yet not heavy, lightly sweetened and very flavorful, perfect with a drizzle of honey or maple syrup.

½ cup (90 g) quinoa, rinsed well and drained

½ cup (80 g) cornmeal

½ cup (75 g) hazelnuts, lightly toasted, skinned, and finely chopped

½ cup (125 ml) milk

3 large eggs, separated

¼ cup (35 g) unbleached all-purpose flour

1 teaspoon fine sea salt

3 tablespoons vanilla sugar (page 10)

Note: *If you omit the sugar, these make a lovely side dish to a main-course salad such as the Butternut Squash and Arugula Salad (page 96).*

I always clean a bowl destined for egg whites with white vinegar before I use it.

1. To toast the quinoa, heat a medium nonstick skillet over medium-high heat. Add the quinoa and cook, stirring slowly and constantly, until it is no longer moist and begins to brown, about 3 minutes. Add 1 cup (250 ml) water and bring to a boil. Reduce the heat to medium-low, cover, and cook until the water is absorbed, about 12 minutes. Uncover and cool.

2. Combine the quinoa, cornmeal, and hazelnuts in a large bowl.

3. In a small bowl, whisk the milk and egg yolks together until blended. Sift the flour and salt onto a piece of wax or parchment paper, then slowly whisk these dry ingredients into the milk mixture. Add the quinoa mixture, stirring until all the ingredients are thoroughly combined.

4. In a separate, clean bowl, whisk the egg whites until they are foamy and beginning to thicken. Slowly add the sugar as you whisk, and continue to whisk until the egg whites form soft peaks. Fold the egg whites gently into the quinoa mixture.

5. Heat a large nonstick griddle or skillet over medium heat until hot enough to sizzle a drop of water. Drop the batter by rounded tablespoons onto the pan. Using the back of the spoon, spread the batter into 2½-inch (6-cm) rounds. Cook until the tops are covered with small bubbles and the bottoms are lightly browned, about 2 minutes. Turn and lightly brown the other side for 2 minutes longer. Keep warm in an oven set at the lowest temperature while you cook the remaining cakes.

Waffles with Walnut Whipped Cream

🌸 *Makes 8 to 12 waffles*

This recipe is a bit of breakfast indulgence, with its fine, fluffy accompaniment of vanilla-laced crème fraîche and walnuts. I like to serve these for a Sunday brunch or for a special occasion such as the first breakfast when company comes to visit or a child's birthday. They're nutty and scrumptious. You can, of course, make the waffles without the topping—they are also delicious on their own.

FOR THE TOPPING:

1 cup (250 ml) crème fraîche

2 tablespoons confectioners' sugar

1 teaspoon vanilla extract

¼ cup (25 g) walnuts, lightly toasted and finely ground

FOR THE WAFFLES:

1½ cups (210 g) unbleached all-purpose flour

1½ teaspoons baking powder

½ teaspoon fine sea salt

3 large eggs, separated

1 cup (250 ml) milk

¼ cup (25 g) walnuts, lightly toasted and finely ground

1 tablespoon vanilla sugar (page 10)

Mild vegetable oil, for oiling the waffle iron

Note: *The recipe calls for walnuts, and they are delicious, but try Brazil nuts or macadamia nuts—they're wonderful as well.*

1. Preheat a waffle iron.

2. Make the topping: Whip the crème fraîche with the confectioners' sugar until the cream holds soft peaks. Fold in the vanilla and ¼ cup (25 g) walnuts. Chill.

3. Sift together the flour, baking powder, and salt. In a large bowl, whisk together the egg yolks and milk. Whisk in the dry ingredients, then whisk in the other ¼ cup (25 g) walnuts.

4. In a large, clean bowl, whisk the egg whites until foamy, then whisk in the vanilla sugar. Continue whisking until the egg whites form soft peaks. Fold the egg whites into the batter.

5. Brush the waffle iron with mild vegetable oil. Place about ⅓ cup batter in the iron and make the waffle according the machine's instructions. Continue until all the batter is used, keeping the waffles warm in a low oven, making sure not to stack them so they do not soften.

6. Serve the waffles with the topping alongside.

Small Plates

Cinnamon Pecans

Lime and Pepper Cashews

Cocoa Nuts with Fleur de Sel

Kaffir Peanuts

Anise- and Fennel-Spiced Walnuts

Salted Spanish Almonds

Toasted Mixed Nuts and Seeds
Fait Maison

Smoked Salmon with Horseradish
Cream and Almonds

Fresh Goat Cheese, Cream,
and Walnut Verrine

Parmigiano-Reggiano Seed Sticks

Muhammara—Heavenly Red
Peppers and Walnuts

Dried Apricot, Lemon, and
Almond Bread

Savory Squash and Cheese Bread

Savory Bread with Sun-Dried
Tomatoes, Pine Nuts, and Pistachios

Dukkah

Walnut and Cheese Crackers

Green Mango or Papaya
Salad—Som Tam

Eggplant with Saffron Walnuts

Brazil Nut Pesto with Pasta

Green Beans, White Peaches,
and Almonds

Avocado with Pistachio Oil and
Chives

Parsley, Green Olive, and
Walnut Salad

Unbeatable Red Beets and Walnuts

Malloreddus de Kita Santa—Tiny
Sardinian Gnocchi for Good Friday

Grilled Vegetable Tarts with
Pumpkin Seeds

Mushroom and Walnut Tarte Tatin

Tomato and Pistachio Croustillant

Fiona's Almond and Olive Sandwich

Almond Soup

Focaccia with Onions and Almonds

Yeast Seed Crackers

Small Plates: Appetizers, First Courses, and Accompaniments

I hope you will turn to this chapter over and over as you plan a meal, for it is rich in the small, simply made, delicious little dishes that make a dining experience special. Dishes like the ones here, rife with nuts and their toasty, buttery flavors and textures, excite the palate and wake it up with flavors that pop with intensity, satisfy with depth.

I often serve a variety of small dishes to introduce a meal. It's a wonderful way to welcome family and friends to the table. Occasionally I offer a larger number of these small dishes as the entire meal, and everyone loves that for its variety and novelty.

Try serving a selection of dishes from this chapter in the kitchen if there is room, with a fire in the fireplace as backdrop, or the doors flung open onto the terrace, or however it strikes you to create a casual, comfortable ambience. I think what you will find, as I do, is that no matter how formal your guests or the occasion, a bounty of small, delicious dishes puts everyone at ease and suddenly, in the way of all that is creative and simple, makes for great company and a wonderful experience.

Cinnamon Pecans

🌸 *Makes about 4 cups (500 g)*

This recipe comes from Sue Raasch, a former cooking student who has a pecan orchard right outside her house in Texas. She made us all laugh with her stories of Texas and of pecans, and the minute she returned home she sent me not only a host of her favorite recipes but also a box of her favorite pecans.

I chose this recipe to represent Sue and pecans. So delicious, so tempting, it is almost too sinful to print. Honestly, these seasoned nuts, which I like to serve as an apéritif, push even the most righteous into decline, for it is impossible to eat just one. They are crisp, they are sweet, they are salty, and they are simply delicious. They will keep, but I doubt that there will ever be, anywhere, any to store.

⅓ cup (65 g) vanilla sugar (page 10)

1 teaspoon ground cinnamon, preferably from Vietnam

1 large egg white

Pinch of fine sea salt

3 cups (350 g) pecans

1 cup (150 g) almonds, coarsely chopped

¼ cup (30 g) sesame seeds

¼ teaspoon fleur de sel

Note: *Stay nearby as these toast, for they can turn the burn corner very quickly.*

1. Preheat the oven to 350°F (180°C).

2. In a small bowl, whisk together the sugar and cinnamon.

3. In a medium bowl, whisk the egg white with the sea salt just until the egg white foams. Add the nuts and sesame seeds and stir to coat. Add the cinnamon sugar mixture and toss with the nuts until they are thoroughly coated. Sprinkle with the fleur de sel. Turn the nuts out onto a jelly-roll pan and toast in the center of the oven until they are golden and smell like heaven, 15 to 20 minutes.

4. Remove the nuts from the oven and let them cool on the pan. They will cool into clumps. To serve, break up the clumps. These nuts will keep in an airtight container for up to 2 weeks. They can also be frozen for up to 2 months.

Lime and Pepper Cashews

🌿 *Makes 2 cups (285 g)*

This recipe was inspired by a delicious salad I had while I was in Thailand. The salad was, quite literally, this mixture atop a bed of fresh, crisp lettuce. Always on the lookout for appetizers, I immediately decided the undressed lettuce was superfluous and this would be a perfect appetizer. I was barely in the door from my trip when I made this, and with its mix of salty, spicy, tangy it was an instant hit.

Note: *The lime juice settles into the cashews over time, softening them just slightly, making leftovers as good as those warm from the oil!*

2 cups (500 ml) mild cooking oil, such as safflower or grapeseed

2 cups (285 g) raw cashews

3 small fresh medium to hot red peppers, thinly sliced

1 tablespoon fresh lime juice

1. Place a sieve over a bowl.

2. Place the oil in a wok or deep saucepan and heat over medium heat to about 375°F (190°C). Add the cashews and cook, stirring constantly, until they are deep golden, about 4 minutes. Using a slotted spoon, transfer the nuts to the sieve. Salt them generously, then toss several times so the salt is well mixed with the nuts. Let the nuts drain in the sieve for at least 10 minutes, then transfer the nuts to a medium bowl and thoroughly toss them with the rounds of pepper. Drizzle the lime juice over the nuts, toss again thoroughly, taste for seasoning, and serve immediately.

3. These will keep for up to 1 week. They don't need to be in an airtight container and, in fact, shouldn't be because they are moist and might mold. Storage is unlikely to be an issue, however, for these do simply disappear!

Cocoa Nuts with Fleur de Sel

🍀 *Makes about 3 cups*

David Lebovitz, pastry chef, cookbook author, and friend, made these for me on one of his visits, and I proceeded to embarrass myself by nibbling away at them as though driven by an unseen force. I had good company, as others in the crowd did the same. These nuts have become part of my repertoire, and I offer the recipe here with David's blessing. I hope that you will pick up and carry the Cocoa Nuts with Fleur de Sel baton, as it deserves to have its message spread throughout the world.

3 cups (about 420 g) raw, very fresh mixed nuts such as cashews, almonds, pecans, hazelnuts

3 tablespoons (45 g) unsalted butter, melted

1 tablespoon aromatic mild honey such as lavender

1 tablespoon dark brown sugar

2 teaspoons unsweetened cocoa powder

¼ teaspoon ground cinnamon

⅛ teaspoon hot paprika

Several grinds of black pepper, preferably Tellicherry

2 tablespoons cocoa nibs (optional)

1 generous teaspoon fleur de sel

Note: *If you cannot find cocoa nibs, don't be concerned. They are a lovely little addition, but the nuts are exquisite without them.*

Move past the nuts' over-roasted appearance, which comes from the cocoa, and get to the heart of the matter. You will understand well and truly that beauty is only skin-deep.

1. Preheat the oven to 350°F (180°C).

2. Spread the nuts in a jelly-roll pan and bake until they begin to smell toasty and turn golden, about 10 minutes. Be very careful as you toast the nuts, and pay attention with your nose as it will tell you when the nuts are perfectly roasted. Remove the nuts from the oven, but leave the oven on.

3. While the nuts are toasting, heat the butter with the honey and brown sugar over low heat in a heavy saucepan large enough to hold the nuts, stirring so that the sugar dissolves. Whisk in the cocoa powder, cinnamon, hot paprika, and pepper and immediately remove from the heat.

4. Add the lightly toasted nuts to the honey mixture, with the cocoa nibs, if using. Mix them gently but thoroughly, using a rubber spatula, until the nuts are coated with the honey mixture and the cocoa nibs are thoroughly incorporated. Fold in the fleur de sel.

5. Spread the nuts evenly in one layer in the pan and return them to the oven. Bake, stirring once or twice, until the nuts are golden and smell toasty, and the glaze is mostly dried and adhering to them, 8 to 10 minutes. Remove from the oven and let the nuts cool.

6. Serve the nuts immediately or store in an airtight container for up to 1 week.

Kaffir Peanuts

🌰 *Makes 2 cups (about 320 g)*

This recipe takes the humble peanut to new heights by removing it from the baseball park or a table in front of the TV and putting it on the dinner table or bar. This is the creation of Andy Ricker, owner of Pok Pok restaurant and whiskey bar in Portland, Oregon, the only authentic Thai street food restaurant on the Pacific Coast of the United States. Kaffir peanuts are salty, they're spicy, they're perfumed, and they are crisp—they'll be gone before you know it.

2 cups (500 ml) mild oil, such as safflower

½ cup gently packed kaffir lime leaves, stemmed

6 whole bird's-eye or Thai chiles

2 cups (320 g) raw red-skinned peanuts

1 teaspoon fine sea salt, or to taste

Note: *Deep-frying peanuts is not hard, but it takes eagle eyes and an attentive nose to survey the heat and remove those peanuts from the fat well before they begin to turn too dark, as they continue to cook once they've left the fat.*

Note, too, that the kaffir lime leaves, which can be found at Asian and international groceries, and peppers are part of the dish, right along with the peanuts.

1. In a wok or smallish deep skillet, heat the oil to 350°F (180°C).

2. Add the kaffir leaves to the oil—be careful, as they will sputter and spit. As soon as all the leaves are in the oil, remove them and drain on paper towels. They will turn slightly golden but should be mostly dark green.

3. Add the chiles to the oil and cook until they are slightly golden, 2 to 3 minutes. Remove from the oil and drain on paper towels.

4. Prepare a sieve by setting it over a medium bowl.

5. Add the peanuts to the oil, turn down the heat slightly, and fry the peanuts until they are light golden, 7 to 8 minutes, stirring occasionally. Every batch of peanuts will fry differently, so you need to stay near them, and if they look and smell as though they are cooking more quickly than indicated, transfer them to the waiting sieve to drain. Blot them gently with paper towels if you feel they have retained too much oil.

6. When the peanuts have cooled but are still quite warm, transfer them to a large bowl. Add the lime leaves, the chiles, and the salt and stir using your hands, breaking up the lime leaves and chiles as you stir. Cover the bowl so it is nearly, but not quite, airtight, and let the peanuts cool to room temperature. Serve immediately.

Anise- and Fennel-Spiced Walnuts

🌶 *Makes about 2 cups (200 g)*

Anise and fennel seeds are an unusual and successful combination with walnuts. Try these for a tasty, toasty accompaniment to champagne or other apéritif. If you have leftovers, they make a fine addition to a green salad or to a dish of freshly steamed seasonal vegetables.

2 teaspoons anise seeds

2 teaspoons fennel seeds

Generous pinch of piment d'Espelette or hot paprika

1 large egg white

Pinch of fine sea salt

2 cups (about 200 g) walnut halves

¼ teaspoon fleur de sel

Note: *Adding a pinch of salt to an egg white helps it to break up more easily. It also seasons the egg white and allows the salt to dissolve before the egg whites foam.*

1. Coarsely crush the anise and fennel seeds using a mortar and pestle. Add the piment d'Espelette or hot paprika and mix well.

2. In a medium bowl, whisk the egg white with the sea salt until foamy. Whisk in the anise mixture. Add the walnut halves and mix well, so the egg white thoroughly coats the walnuts. If there is excess egg white on the walnuts, set a fine-mesh sieve over a large bowl, place the walnut halves in the sieve, and let the excess egg white drain off the walnuts. This may take 10 to 15 minutes.

3. Place the walnut halves in a nonstick skillet and then place the skillet over medium heat. Sauté the walnut halves until they are pale golden on all sides and smell deliciously toasty, 8 to 10 minutes. Add the fleur de sel and toss the walnuts, then transfer them to a cooling rack or a wooden cutting board to cool. Serve when the nuts are cool. These walnuts will keep well for up to 1 month, if stored in an airtight container in a cool, dark spot. They do not need refrigeration.

Salted Spanish Almonds

🌿 *Makes 2 cups (270 g)*

Spanish almonds, the best of which are the flat, crisp Marcona variety, have an intense yet delicate almond flavor. In Spain they are deep-fried or roasted and salted and served as a snack, or they are toasted and used to adorn sweets. Here I've taken the Marcona almond, salted it, and baked it in the oven, to give it a thorough pale golden crunch with a peppery edge.

1. Preheat the oven to 325°F (165°C). Line a cooling rack with parchment paper.

2. Place 2 cups (500 ml) water, the salt, and the hot paprika in a medium, heavy saucepan over medium-high heat. When the salt has dissolved, add the almonds, stir, and boil until the almonds begin to look translucent, about 8 minutes. Drain the almonds and spread them evenly on a nonreactive baking sheet. Bake in the center of the oven until the almonds are pale golden and crisp, 20 to 30 minutes. Do not let the almonds get toasty brown as that will dull their delicate flavor.

3. Remove the almonds from the oven and transfer them to the prepared rack. Let them cool entirely before serving. These will keep in an airtight container for about 2 weeks or in the freezer for about 3 months.

2 tablespoons coarse sea salt

½ teaspoon hot paprika

2 cups (270 g) Spanish almonds, blanched

Toasted Mixed Nuts and Seeds Fait Maison

🍀 *Makes 6 cups (1.5 kg)*

Toasted nuts are easy to find on a supermarket shelf, but they are almost as easy to make yourself. Toasting your own nuts is like sustainable farming—you're on top of the whole process, from start to finish. You may not produce the nuts, but you carefully purchase them, decide how to season them, watch them as they toast, then finally add other ingredients that you like. With minimal effort you'll have the best toasted nuts on the block.

1 cup (150 g) hazelnuts

1 cup (150 g) almonds

½ cup (50 g) walnuts

1 cup (140 g) cashews

½ cup (70 g) sunflower seeds

½ cup (70 g) pumpkin seeds

1 to 2 tablespoons extra virgin olive oil

Scant teaspoon fine sea salt

1 cup (150 g) raisins (optional)

Note: *The raisins are optional. I like a touch of sweet in my salted nuts when I'm reserving them for a snack, but if I'm serving toasted nuts as an apéritif, I prefer to leave out the raisins.*

The hazelnuts are toasted separately so their skins can be removed.

1. Preheat the oven to 375°F (190°C).

2. Place the hazelnuts on a baking dish in the oven and toast them until they are golden and begin to scent the kitchen, 8 to 10 minutes. Remove from the oven and transfer them to a tea towel. Fold the tea towel over the hazelnuts and let them sit for about 10 minutes. Vigorously rub the hazelnuts in the tea towel to remove the skin and discard the papery skins.

3. Place the remaining nuts and seeds in a large bowl. Drizzle with the olive oil and toss, then sprinkle with the salt and toss so the salt is mixed evenly among the nuts. Place the nuts in a baking dish and roast until they are

golden, which will take 10 to 12 minutes. Remove the nuts from the oven and transfer them to a sieve so they can cool without sweating.

4. When the nuts are cool, toss them with the hazelnuts and raisins if you like and store in an airtight container in a cool, dry place for up to 1 month.

· ·

Nutcrackers

According to excavations done in the United States and Europe, cavepeople went after nuts with hollowed-out stones. It was the Germans who christened the popular nutcracker, or *nut biter* as they called it, by making it move and, later, giving it a heart and soul.

The woodcarvers of the Thüringen toy industry carved nutcrackers in the shape of small figures—policemen, foresters, soldiers, and a variety of animals—with two moving levers on the back of the head that caused the jaws to crack the nut against each other. Another German, E.T.A. Hoffmann, gave life to the nutcracker in his *Nussknacker und Mausekönig*, or *The Nutcracker and the Mouse King*.

"Under the Christmas tree a very excellent little man became visible that stood there still and modestly. He waited as if they would all come to him," Hoffmann wrote.

Tchaikovsky's *Nutcracker Suite*, based on Hoffmann's story, turned the nutcracker into royalty as he became not only a prince but also a girl's best friend.

From nut biter to best friend, the nutcracker will, no doubt, always hold a place in our kitchen drawer, as well as in our hearts.

Smoked Salmon with Horseradish Cream and Almonds

❧ *Makes 6 servings*

This lovely little appetizer was inspired by a meal I had at a tapas restaurant in Paris. I loved the blend of silken and crunchy and the idea that salmon would be good with something other than a slice of fresh lemon. Everything about this dish speaks of subtlety, including the drizzle of almond oil tossed with the salmon. If you don't have almond oil, use a lightly fruity extra virgin olive oil instead.

4 ounces (120 g) smoked salmon, lox style, preferably without nitrates

1 teaspoon almond oil

One 2-inch (5-cm) piece cucumber, peeled, seeded, and cut into tiny dice

One 7-inch (18-cm) celery stalk, strings removed , cut into tiny dice

2 tablespoons fresh dill, chopped

1 tablespoon sliced almonds

4 small radicchio leaves, cut into very thin strips (chiffonade)

FOR THE HORSERADISH CREAM:

Generous ¼ cup (60 ml) heavy non-ultrapasteurized cream

2 teaspoons creamy-style horseradish

Note: *The recipe calls for ingredients cut into tiny dice. Tiny is what you are after here, as the small size of the vegetables gives a little point of flavor to the dish.*

You can make the elements of this dish several hours in advance, but assemble it right before serving so that all of the flavors retain their texture and intensity. Make sure the toasted almonds are thoroughly cool before adding them to the dish.

If you have a leftover serving or two, it makes a delicious sandwich filling.

1. Slice the salmon, with the grain, into very thin (barely ¼-inch/.6-cm) slices. Place the salmon in a medium bowl, add the almond oil, and toss. Add the cucumber, celery, dill, almonds, and radicchio to the salmon and fold the ingredients together. Either refrigerate immediately or evenly divide the salmon mixture among six wineglasses or other small glass bowls or cups.

2. For the topping, place the cream in a large bowl and whisk it until it forms soft peaks. Whisk in the

¼ teaspoon fresh lemon juice

2 tablespoons sliced almonds,
lightly toasted

horseradish and lemon juice. Taste for seasoning. Evenly divide the cream mixture among the glasses, spooning it atop the salmon. Sprinkle each serving with an equal amount of the toasted almonds and serve immediately or refrigerate for up to 1 hour.

Fresh Goat Cheese, Cream, and Walnut Verrine

🍀 *Makes 6 servings*

Verrine is a combination of the word *terrine*, which is similar to a pâté made with either vegetables, seafood, or meat (*terrine* also refers to the rectangular mold the mixture is cooked in), and the word *verre*, or glass.

I first encountered verrines at the restaurant of Nicolas Le Bec in Lyon, where many dishes are served in jars and other unusual containers. Here's a summery verrine that I came up with that uses fresh goat cheese, tomatoes bursting with flavor, and mint leaves. Serve this as suggested, in fanciful glasses as a first course, or even as a between-courses taste.

8 ounces (225 g) soft fresh goat cheese

1 small shallot, minced

Fine sea salt and freshly ground black pepper

⅓ cup (80 ml) heavy non-ultrapasteurized cream, chilled

2 medium (5-ounce/150-g) very ripe and flavorful tomatoes, peeled, seeded, and diced

2 teaspoons walnut oil

¼ cup (25 g) walnuts, lightly toasted and finely minced

Fresh mint leaves or chervil for garnish

Note: *If you cannot find fresh goat cheese, which is soft and almost a bit wet, use large-curd cottage cheese with a bit of yogurt stirred into it, pureed in a blender.*

You may prepare the elements of this dish several hours in advance, up to putting the tomatoes in the glasses. But assemble them no sooner than half an hour before you plan to serve them.

1. In a small bowl or the bowl of a food processor, puree the goat cheese until it is smooth. Transfer the goat cheese to a small bowl and fold in the shallot. Season to taste with salt and pepper.

2. Whisk the cream to stiff peaks. Fold it into the seasoned goat cheese.

3. Place the tomatoes in a small bowl with the walnut oil and toss until they are coated. Season with salt and pepper. Place an equal amount of seasoned tomatoes in the bottom of six martini or other nicely shaped glasses. Top with 1 teaspoon of the toasted walnuts, then with equal amounts of goat cheese. Sprinkle the remaining toasted walnuts over each serving. Serve immediately, garnished with the mint leaves or chervil.

Parmigiano-Reggiano Seed Sticks

🌱 *Makes about 50*

These are the first appetizer to disappear at a party. They're easy to make and best to serve when they are still lukewarm and fresh from the oven. If you do have leftovers, give them a little heat to re-crisp them before serving.

1 cup (140 g) all-purpose flour

Pinch of fine sea salt

¼ cup (60 g) Dukkah (page 50)

4 ounces (110 g) Parmigiano-Reggiano, finely grated

7 tablespoons (100 g) unsalted butter, cut into 14 pieces, chilled

FOR THE GLAZE:

1 small egg

Note: *I like to roll out these little sticks and refrigerate them, then put them in the oven right before my guests arrive. That way they bake and cool just to the perfect temperature in time for serving, and they make the kitchen smell like heaven. Serve these with a lovely dry sherry.*

1. Place the flour, salt, dukkah, and Parmigiano-Reggiano in a food processor and pulse once to mix. Add the butter and process until the mixture resembles coarse meal, pulsing five to eight times. Add 5 tablespoons (75 ml) ice water and pulse just until the pastry begins to hold together and is quite damp. Add another table-spoon of water if the pastry seems dry.

2. Turn the pastry out of the food processor onto your work surface and form it into a flat round. Let it rest on the work surface at room temperature, covered with a tea towel or a bowl, for 30 to 60 minutes.

3. Preheat the oven to 425°F (220°C).

4. Roll out the pastry to a ⅛-inch-thick rectangle. Mix the egg with 1 teaspoon water and brush the pastry with the egg glaze. Then cut it into 4 × ½-inch (10 × 1.25-cm)

strips. Transfer the strips to a baking sheet and bake in the center of the oven until the pastry is crisp, 10 to 12 minutes. Remove from the oven and transfer to a cooling rack to cool. Serve immediately.

Muhammara—Heavenly Red Peppers and Walnuts

🌿 *Makes a generous 2 cups (500 g)*

I ate this marvelous mixture—which is similar to a sunset-hued tapenade, only sweeter—in southeastern Turkey every chance I got, which was often. It is served for breakfast, lunch, and dinner, always accompanied by the region's pillowy bread. What I learned in Turkey was that any cook worth his or her salt has a personal recipe for muhammara, of which each is extremely proud. Some versions are spicy, some are sweeter than others, all are ripe and full with the flavor of the region's special bell-shaped peppers and crisp, buttery walnuts.

This recipe is an adaptation of one I enjoyed from the hands of Sermin Ocak, the recognized matron of gastronomy in the city of Gaziantep. Mrs. Ocak was asked by the mayor of Gaziantep to prepare a meal of all the region's favorite dishes, and this was among the first (of dozens) she served. To make her version, which is more vividly red than many, Mrs. Ocak uses her home-dried peppers, which she reconstitutes overnight in water and then grinds to a paste. The result of her care is muhammara that sings with the flavor—and the culture and the wealth—of Gaziantep.

On my last morning in Gaziantep, my host, Filiz Hosokuglu, served her mother's version of muhammara. Darker red than this version, it was heartier in flavor but equally smooth and delicious. We ate it on fresh bread, along with a bowl of steaming coffee. Mmmm!

When I serve muhammara now, I offer it as an appetizer along with raw vegetables and fresh bread. It is also wonderful spread on pizza dough, which is then baked and garnished with extra virgin olive oil.

1¾ cups (175 g) walnuts

1½ pounds (680 g) red bell peppers (3 large or 5 small),

Note: *Muhammara is very good served with Yeast Seed Crackers (page 81).*

1. Place the walnuts in a food processor and pulse sev-

roasted (page 94), peeled, and seeded

1 tablespoon tomato paste

¾ cup (60 g) fresh bread crumbs

¼ cup (60 ml) extra virgin olive oil

1 tablespoon fresh lemon juice

1 teaspoon coarsely ground Aleppo pepper or mild paprika

1 teaspoon cumin seeds, lightly toasted and coarsely ground

Fine sea salt

eral times, until they are coarsely ground. Add the peppers and pulse several times. Scrape down the sides of the bowl and add the tomato paste, bread crumbs, olive oil, lemon juice, Aleppo pepper, cumin, and salt to taste. Process to make a coarse paste, scraping down the processor from time to time. Season to taste with salt. Serve immediately or store in an airtight container in the refrigerator for at least 1 week.

The "green germ" of the garlic is the nascent garlic plant, trying its best to grow from within the garlic clove. When you cut a garlic clove in half, lengthwise, you can see the germ of the garlic. If it is early in the season—from the end of July when garlic is harvested, usually through October—the germ is barely formed, and if it is there, it will be the same color as the garlic clove. You don't need to remove it, and can chop with impunity. When the germ is green, it should be removed because it's texture is soft and can be stringy, and it adds nothing to a dish. Some say it can be bitter and can cause gastric upset, but I have never experienced either of these phenomena.

Dried Apricot, Lemon, and Almond Bread

🍀 *Makes 10 to 12 servings*

This wonderful sweet and savory bread, called a "cake" in France, was inspired by one I tasted at the *salon de thé* in the garden of the Musée de la Vie Romantique in Paris. Chef and owner Didier Bertrand gave me his recipe, and I tweaked it just slightly until it came out, to my taste, perfect. I do as the French do and serve this cake cut into small slices as an apéritif, with a glass of chilled Savennières or a flute of champagne.

1½ cups (200 g) unbleached all-purpose flour

1 tablespoon baking powder

1 mounded teaspoon fine sea salt

6 large eggs

Mounded ¼ teaspoon freshly ground black pepper

8 tablespoons (1 stick/110 g) unsalted butter, melted and cooled

8 dried apricots (7 ounces/210 g), coarsely chopped

6 ounces (180 g) Gruyère or Emmental cheese, finely grated (2 cups)

½ teaspoon fennel seeds, crushed

Zest of 1 lemon, coarsely chopped

Generous ¼ cup (about 60 g) almonds, lightly toasted, chopped

Note: *Try to find unsulphured apricots for this bread—dark and plump, they offer a true apricot flavor.*

1. Preheat the oven to 425°F (220°C). Butter a loaf pan. Line it with parchment paper, butter the parchment paper, and dust it lightly with flour.

2. Sift the flour, baking powder, and salt onto another piece of parchment paper.

3. In a large bowl or the bowl of an electric mixer, whisk the eggs until they are broken up and blended, then slowly whisk in the dry ingredients and the black pepper. Stir in the melted butter until it is thoroughly blended, then fold in the apricots, cheese, fennel seeds, lemon zest, and almonds, making sure the nuts are well distributed throughout the batter.

4. Pour the batter into the prepared pan, rap it sharply on a work surface to release any air bubbles, and bake in the center of the oven until the top of the bread is golden and a sharp knife stuck in the center comes out clean, 40 to 45 minutes.

5. Remove the bread from the oven and turn it out onto a wire cooling rack. After about 10 minutes, peel off the parchment paper. Let it cool and serve. This bread will keep for up to 3 days, carefully wrapped. Don't refrigerate it, as refrigeration dries it out.

Savory Squash and Cheese Bread

🌿 *Makes 8 to 10 servings*

The texture of this savory *gâteau de potimarron au Comté* lies somewhere between that of a crustless quiche and the Savory Bread with Sun-Dried Tomatoes, Pine Nuts, and Pistachios that follows. It makes a wonderful accompaniment to a rich white wine, such as one from Château Turcaud, sliced into thick slices, then cut in half on the diagonal.

This makes a lovely appetizer, but it is also a good main-course lunch dish, with a crisp green salad alongside. Some of my friends serve it as a vegetable, too, alongside a steak or lamb chop from the grill.

2 pounds (1 kg) kuri squash, peeled, seeded, and cut into 2-inch (5-cm) chunks (2 rounded cups cooked squash)

3 large eggs

2 tablespoons heavy non-ultrapasteurized cream

½ cup (125 ml) milk

3 tablespoons unbleached all-purpose flour

¼ teaspoon fine sea salt

5 ounces (150 g) Comté or other hard Swiss-type cheese, grated

1 tablespoon pine nut oil or extra virgin olive oil

¼ cup (30 g) pine nuts, toasted

Several grinds of white pepper

Note: *Use kuri or another very firm squash, such as butternut. A watery squash like pumpkin won't work, unless you are willing to cook all the liquid from it once it is steamed.*

1. Preheat the oven to 400°F (200°C). Butter a loaf pan and line it with parchment paper.

2. Bring 3 cups water to a boil in the bottom half of a steamer or in a saucepan fitted with a collapsible steamer. Steam the squash in the top until it is tender through, about 15 minutes. Remove from the steamer and place the squash in a large bowl. Using a potato ricer or masher, mash the squash until it is nearly completely smooth. Do not be concerned if there are some small lumps.

3. Whisk the eggs with the cream and milk in a medium bowl. Whisk in the flour and salt, then fold in the grated cheese. Stir this mixture slowly into the squash just until all the ingredients are combined. Fold in the oil, half the toasted pine nuts, and the pepper. Taste the mixture and adjust the seasoning if necessary.

4. Pour the squash mixture into the prepared loaf pan. Top with the remaining pine nuts. Bake in the center of the oven until the bread is firm to the touch and a knife inserted in the center comes out clean, about 1 hour. Remove from the oven and cool to room temperature, then turn out of the pan. To serve, cut into thick slices, then cut each slice in half on the diagonal. This will keep for up to 2 days, wrapped well and refrigerated.

Savory Bread with Sun-Dried Tomatoes, Pine Nuts, and Pistachios

❧ *Makes 1 loaf; 10 to 12 appetizer servings*

A friend of mine, Marie Boivin, who is also part of a wine-tasting group that meets monthly at my home, brought this one evening, and it was the hit of the soirée. Savory and tart, tender and toothsome, it is such a very French appetizer. Appetizers like this were all the rage in France in the 1960s, and while they've never gone away, they are currently experiencing something of a revival. There are so many variations on the theme, and every now and then one of them is exceptional, like this one.

1½ cups (200 g) unbleached all-purpose flour

Rounded ¼ teaspoon fine sea salt

1 tablespoon baking powder

6 large eggs

1 tablespoon Dijon mustard

8 tablespoons (125 g) unsalted butter, melted

8 sun-dried tomatoes, finely chopped

¼ cup (45 g) pistachios, lightly toasted

¼ cup (40 g) pine nuts, lightly toasted

¼ cup (40 g) pumpkin seeds, lightly toasted

3 ounces (90 g) Parmigiano-Reggiano, finely grated

Note: *You may also add thin strips of prosciutto or other air-cured ham to this bread.*

Also, if you want to serve this as a dressed-up accompaniment to an apéritif, slice it, then slice each slice into four diamond shapes and arrange them on a platter or plate. That way they are a handy, savory little mouthful.

If you have very dry sun-dried tomatoes, you may want to plump them slightly by steaming them, then carefully pat them dry.

1. Preheat the oven to 425°F (220°C). Line a loaf pan with parchment paper. Lightly butter the parchment paper. Preheat the oven to 350°F (180°C).

2. Sift the flour, salt, and baking powder onto another piece of parchment paper.

3. In a large bowl or the bowl of an electric mixer, whisk the eggs just until they are broken up. Whisk in the mustard, then quickly whisk in the dry ingredients. Fold in the melted butter, then the tomatoes, nuts, seeds, and cheese until thoroughly combined.

4. Turn the batter into the prepared pan. Bake in the center of the oven until the bread is golden on top and a knife inserted in the center comes out clean, about 45 minutes.

5. Remove the bread from the oven and turn it out onto a wire cooling rack. After about 5 minutes, peel off the parchment paper. Let the bread cool before serving.

Dukkah

Dukkah was one of those words I kept hearing from my cooking students during the spring of 2007, when this savory mixture was just becoming popular in the United States. Everyone seemed to be sprinkling this savory, spicy, crunchy, nutty mixture atop everything. I'd forgotten about it until I went to the Portland, Oregon, farmers' market and discovered Oregon Dukkah, a company devoted to making delicious dukkah from Oregon hazelnuts.

I was delighted to find dukkah, and more delighted at the possibilities it offers. Now that I have it in my repertoire I use it on many things—to liven up a salad, to sprinkle on steamed vegetables or fish, to fold into bread or pastry dough. One of my favorite ways to serve it, and one that surprises and pleases, is as an impromptu apéritif along with freshly baked bread and raw seasonal vegetables and a dish of exceptional extra virgin olive oil. Dip the bread and/or vegetable in oil, then dip in dukkah. You won't stop!

¾ cup (115 g) hazelnuts

½ cup (70 g) sesame seeds

3 tablespoons coriander seeds

3 tablespoons cumin seeds

1½ teaspoons fine sea salt

2 tablespoons coarsely ground
    black pepper

1 teaspoon hot or mild paprika

Note: *Try adding dukkah to bread dough, or slipping it under the skin of a chicken before roasting.*

1. Preheat the oven to 350°F (180°C).

2. Toast the hazelnuts in a pan in the oven until they begin to turn golden and smell toasty, about 8 minutes. Remove from the oven and transfer to a paper bag or a tea towel, which you must close around the nuts so they steam slightly and their skins blister away from the nuts. Note that hazelnuts tend to roast unevenly, and you may need to return some of them to the oven to continue roasting. When the nuts are cool, rub them in the towel or bag to remove as much of the papery skin as possible.

3. Place the sesame seeds in a pan and roast them in

the oven until they begin to smell toasty, about 8 minutes. Check them often, as they have a tendency to toast very suddenly. Remove from the oven and cool.

4. Place the coriander seeds in a small skillet over medium heat and sauté just until they begin to smell fragrant, about 1 minute. Remove from the heat. Repeat with the cumin seeds.

5. Place the hazelnuts, sesame seeds, and salt in a food processor and pulse until the nuts are coarsely chopped. Add the coriander and cumin seeds, pepper, and paprika and process until the mixture is finely ground. Be careful not to overprocess so the nuts don't become oily. Taste for seasoning—you may want to add more salt. Transfer to a serving bowl and serve immediately or store in an airtight container in a cool dark spot for up to 2 weeks or indefinitely in the freezer.

Walnut and Cheese Crackers

🦋 *Makes about thirty-six 4½×2½-inch (11×6-cm) crackers*

These will remind you of Cheez-Its, those bright orange squares some of us loved as kids, though these are so, so much better! Here, walnuts provide a nutty flavor that is balanced by the cheese and butter. These are delicious as appetizers—try them with some thinly sliced cucumber and a bit of cumin salt (page 226) or gomasio (page 227). Make a bit of yogurt cheese, add some to a cracker, and top with thinly sliced vegetables or halved cherry tomatoes. These also make a great after-school snack.

1½ cups (200 g) unbleached all-purpose flour

¾ cup (100 g) whole wheat flour

1 teaspoon fine sea salt

½ teaspoon baking powder

7 tablespoons (105 g) unsalted butter, cut into about 10 pieces, at room temperature

⅓ cup (35 g) walnuts, finely ground

5 ounces (150 g) Parmigiano-Reggiano, finely grated (to give 2 cups)

1 medium egg

Note: *Be sure to let the dough rest the required amount of time so the gluten in the flour has time to relax, resulting in tender crackers.*

1. Place the flours, salt, and baking powder in a large bowl or the bowl of an electric mixer or food processor and mix with the paddle attachment. Add the butter and mix until the butter is incorporated into the flour so the mixture looks a bit like coarse cornmeal. This will take some time in an electric mixer; be patient! It will be quicker in a food processor, and it is possible to do it by hand as well, by rubbing the butter into the dry ingredients with your fingertips. Add the walnuts and cheese and mix just until combined.

2. Whisk the egg with 3 tablespoons water and add it to the mixture ingredients with the mixer on. If using a mixer, the dough may clump on the paddle, so stop the machine, remove the clump of dough, and continue mixing, adding ½ cup (125 ml) water 1 tablespoon at a time until the dough holds together. If the dough is dry and crumbly, add additional water, 1 tablespoon at a time, until it holds together.

3. Let the dough rest, covered, for 30 to 60 minutes.

4. Preheat the oven to 375°F (190°C). Line two or three baking sheets with parchment paper.

5. Lightly flour a work surface. Working with half the dough, roll it out as thin as you can, 1/8 to 1/4 inch (.3 to .6 cm) thick. Cut the dough into strips 2 inches (5 cm) wide, then cut the strips the length you'd like them. Transfer the pieces of dough to the prepared baking sheets, arranging them so they are almost touching, as they will not expand during baking. Bake in the center of the oven until they are pale gold and cooked through, which will take 15 to 18 minutes. Be careful not to overbake them, as they can become bitter. Transfer them to a wire cooling rack to cool, and when they are completely cooled, either serve them immediately or store them in an airtight container. They will keep well for about 10 days.

Green Mango or Papaya Salad—Som Tam

I had not been in Chiang Mai, Thailand, for more than ten minutes before I was speeding down side roads, over the Ping River, through harsh sunlight and down a dusty street where my friend and guide, Sunny Bovormat, screeched to a halt. With Andy Ricker, Thai food expert, we descended from the car and entered a lush, breezy world. It was a wonderfully cool restaurant with a thatched roof, no walls, and three kitchens, each responsible for something different. The green papaya salad kitchen, which was near the grilled meats section, was the busiest, the "pok pok" of the mortar and pestle the background music to the ambience. My two expert guides ordered som tam the way they wanted it, for in Thai restaurants it is the client who creates the recipe. I loved my hosts' choice, and this is their recipe.

3 small garlic cloves, peeled

1 fresh or dried Thai chile, seeded if desired and cut into 1-inch (2.5-cm) lengths

2 tablespoons palm sugar

1 teaspoon dried shrimp, rinsed

1 long bean, cut into 1-inch (2.5-cm) pieces, or 3 standard green beans, trimmed

1 tablespoon fresh lime juice

1 tablespoon fish sauce, preferably Thai

2 small green mangoes or papayas, peeled and shredded (1½ cups/375 ml)

Note: *I call for either green mangoes or papaya here. You may actually use any vegetable mixed with either of the two or, if you cannot find a green papaya or mango, substitute grated unripe pear or an unripe apple—something crisp and tart.*

All of the Asian ingredients can be found at Asian markets and many supermarkets.

1. Place the garlic, chile, and palm sugar in a mortar and grind them together until they make a paste. Add the dried shrimp and pound them until they break apart. Add the long bean and just crush it with the pestle, then stir in the lime juice and fish sauce.

2. Add the shredded mango and pound it just slightly into the sauce ingredients, then continue mixing using

6 cherry tomatoes, halved

1 heaping tablespoon peanuts, lightly toasted and coarsely chopped

two forks until all the ingredients are combined. Stir in the tomatoes and peanuts and taste for seasoning. Transfer the mixture to a shallow serving bowl and serve immediately, making sure that each guest gets some of the dressing and the juice that the green mango will give up.

Eggplant with Saffron Walnuts

❧ *Makes 6 servings*

Walnuts, eggplant, saffron, and fresh herbs are combined in this rustic dish. Make it at the height of summer when eggplant is plentiful. Serve it warm or at room temperature as a first course, alongside grilled fish or meat as a side dish, or as the main course of a vegetarian meal.

⅓ cup (80 ml) extra virgin olive oil

1 scant teaspoon saffron threads

3 tablespoons fresh lemon juice

3 medium eggplants (about 1½ pounds/625 g), cut lengthwise into ½-inch (1.25-cm) thick slices

Sea salt

1 generous pound (520 g) onions, diced

3 large garlic cloves, minced

¾ cup (75 g) walnuts, lightly toasted and minced

2 cups (20 g) gently packed flat-leaf parsley leaves

¾ cup (8 g) gently packed cilantro leaves

¾ cup (8 g) gently packed basil leaves

Freshly ground black pepper

Fleur de sel

Note: *Oven baking, rather than frying, softens the eggplant, and economizes on the amount of oil used.*

Note, too, that eggplant needs salting to remove bitterness if it isn't freshly harvested. If you find a firm, shiny-skinned, fresh-from-the-farm or -garden eggplant, there's no need to salt it.

1. Preheat the oven to 450°F (230°C). Brush two baking sheets each with 2 to 3 teaspoons olive oil. Place the saffron in a small dish and cover with 1 tablespoon of the lemon juice. Reserve.

2. Place the eggplant slices on the prepared baking sheets, then brush each slice with olive oil, using about 1 tablespoon altogether. Sprinkle the slices lightly with sea salt and bake until they are golden and slightly softened, about 10 minutes. Turn the slices, season lightly with salt, and continue baking until they are tender through but not dry, 10 to 15 minutes longer. Remove from the oven.

3. While the eggplant are cooking, place 2 tablespoons of the remaining olive oil and the onions in a large, heavy skillet over medium heat and cook, stirring occasionally, until the onions are beginning to soften, about 8 minutes. Add the garlic, stir, and cook until the garlic has softened,

4 to 5 minutes. Add the walnuts, the saffron with its lemon juice, and the remaining lemon juice and cook, stirring, until the lemon juice has evaporated and the onions are soft through, 4 to 5 minutes. Remove from the heat.

4. Mince the herbs and stir them into the onion and walnut mixture until the ingredients are thoroughly combined. Season to taste with sea salt and pepper.

5. Spread 2 tablespoons of the onion and walnut mixture on the wider end of each of the eggplant slices, then fold the narrower end over the stuffing and press the eggplant gently down over the filling, to form a small packet. Arrange the packets on a warmed serving platter. Drizzle the packets with the remaining olive oil, then top with any remaining stuffing. Season with fleur de sel and serve hot or at room temperature.

Brazil Nut Pesto with Pasta

🌿 *Makes ¾ cup (185 ml)*

The crisp crunch of Brazil nuts yields an unexpected pesto. A delicate anise flavor from the basil makes it familiar, yet the herbal zest of flat-leaf parsley adds a new dimension. This pesto can be used like any other—on pasta, under the skin of chicken destined for roasting, as a dip for raw vegetables, slathered on pizza hot from the oven. It fits into a meal in just about any spot but dessert!

½ cup (75 g) Brazil nuts, coarsely chopped

1 large garlic clove, coarsely chopped

2 cups (20 g) gently packed flat-leaf parsley leaves

1 cup (10 g) basil leaves

½ teaspoon finely grated lemon zest

7 tablespoons (105 ml) extra virgin olive oil

1 ounce (30 g) Parmigiano-Reggiano, finely grated

Fine sea salt

1 pound (500 g) dried penne or fusilli pasta or any fanciful shape that will grab the pesto

Note: *Only half of the pesto is used here, so you will have some left over to use as you like.*

1. Place the nuts and the garlic in a food processor or in a mortar and pulse or crush until they are coarsely chopped. Add the herbs and lemon zest and process or pound until all are blended into a relatively smooth but still somewhat chunky mixture. With the food processor running, or stirring with a pestle, slowly add the olive oil until it is combined with the herbs and nuts.

2. Transfer the mixture to a small bowl and stir in the Parmigiano-Reggiano until thoroughly combined. Season with salt if necessary and reserve.

3. Bring a large pot of generously salted water to a boil over medium-high heat.

4. Place the pasta in the salted water and cook just until al dente, about 7 minutes. Drain, reserving some of the cooking water. Transfer the pasta to a large bowl

and stir in half the pesto. Taste for seasoning and moisture. If you want the pasta with a more intense pesto
flavor, add additional pesto. If the pasta is dry, add some
of the cooking water, 1 tablespoon at a time, until the
pasta is moist enough to suit you. Serve immediately.

Green Beans, White Peaches, and Almonds

Credit for this dish goes to Chef Alain Passard of the restaurant Arpège, in Paris, where I tasted it some years ago. What I loved most about it were the immature green almonds sprinkled on top. They are the perfect, tender-crisp foil for the juicy white peaches and succulent green beans, an unusual little element whose delicacy is echoed with almond oil on the green beans and in the vinaigrette.

Come midsummer, green almonds are in the marketplace, hidden in their furry green shells. They are soft, juicy, and tender for just a moment before they begin to toughen up, develop their brown skin, and turn into the almonds we all know.

FOR THE GREEN BEANS:

2 pounds (1 kg) green beans, trimmed

3 tablespoons almond oil

FOR THE VINAIGRETTE:

1 tablespoon raspberry vinegar

¼ teaspoon fine sea salt, or to taste

1 large shallot, minced

3 tablespoons almond oil

1 tablespoon extra virgin olive oil

Freshly ground black pepper

Note: *Green almonds are available by mail order from www.greenalmonds.com. If you miss the season and want to make this salad, use regular, blanched almonds.*

1. Bring 3 cups (750 ml) water to a boil in the bottom of a steamer. Steam the green beans until they are tender through but still a vivid green, 8 to 10 minutes. Transfer the beans to a large bowl and toss them with the almond oil. Reserve.

2. In a medium bowl, whisk together the vinegar and the salt. Add the shallot, whisk, then slowly whisk in the oils. Season lightly with the pepper.

3. Cut each peach into thin wedges. Add the peaches to the raspberry vinaigrette and toss gently.

FOR THE PEACHES:

2 pounds (1 kg) white peaches, peeled and pitted

Sea salt and freshly ground black pepper

¾ cup (120 g) shelled green almonds (about 1½ pounds/625 g in the shell)

4. To assemble the salad, evenly divide the beans among six serving plates. Top each plate with an equal amount of peaches. Dust with sea salt and black pepper. Sprinkle with the almonds and serve immediately.

Avocado with Pistachio Oil and Chives

Simple and pure, this is the perfect combination of ingredients. I use pistachio oil produced in Burgundy by the Leblanc family, which is like an elixir filled with the flavor of the best Turkish pistachio nuts, lightly toasted, carefully pressed. You can order Leblanc pistachio oil from ingoodtastestore.com, and I suggest you do so. It is well worth it. Otherwise, substitute the best possible extra virgin olive oil and use 3 tablespoons of pistachio nuts.

4 avocados, peeled, pitted, and cut into 12 slices each

1 small bunch of chives

3 tablespoons pistachio oil

Fleur de sel

2 tablespoons pistachio nuts, salted or unsalted, lightly toasted and minced

4 chive blossoms or any small, edible flower

Note: *To choose a perfect avocado, test it very gently—it should have the same firmness as the end of your nose, firm but with a bit of give.*

If you have an abundance of avocados, refrigerate them; they will keep well in the refrigerator for up to a week.

1. Arrange 8 avocado slices on each of six plates, fanning them out nicely.

2. Mince the chives and, in a small bowl, mix them with the pistachio oil. Drizzle the mixture evenly over the avocado slices and season with fleur de sel.

3. Evenly sprinkle the minced pistachios over the avocado.

4. Separate the individual blossoms from the chive flowers and sprinkle them over the avocado. Serve immediately.

Parsley, Green Olive, and Walnut Salad

🍀 *Makes 6 servings*

I remember the way my mouth filled with the bright, green herbal flavor of parsley when I ate this salad at a restaurant in Gaziantep, Turkey. Bright and flavorful, it manages to be delicious and feel healthy and cleansing at the same time.

In Gaziantep, this salad is the traditional accompaniment for the city's noted kebabs, which are grilled over coals. I like to serve this with any grilled meat or fish, or as a first course to introduce a meal of roasted meat, fish, or poultry.

Note: *If you cannot find pomegranate molasses (it is available at Middle Eastern groceries), substitute balsamic vinegar, although it doesn't have the syrupy, tart depth of the pomegranate molasses.*

A little note on pitting olives: You can use an olive or cherry pitter, but a more efficient method is to place several olives in a row on a work surface and smack them lightly but firmly with the flat side of a knife. The olives will burst, releasing their pits, which are then easy to pop out.

1. Place the scallions, bell pepper, parsley leaves, green olives, and walnuts in a medium bowl and toss. In another bowl, whisk together the lemon juice, pomegranate molasses, salt, pepper, and olive oil until thoroughly combined.

2. Pour the dressing over the salad ingredients and toss until thoroughly coated. Evenly divide the salad among six salad plates. Garnish each salad with the pomegranate seeds if desired. Serve immediately.

- 3 scallions, trimmed and cut into paper-thin rounds (⅓ cup)
- 1 small (4.5-ounce/135 g) red bell pepper, seeds and white pith removed, cut into very thin strips
- 3 cups (30 g) gently packed flat-leaf parsley leaves
- 1½ cups (230 g) brined green olives, pitted and coarsely chopped
- ⅓ cup (35 g) raw walnuts, coarsely chopped
- 1 tablespoon freshly squeezed lemon juice
- 1 teaspoon pomegranate molasses or balsamic vinegar
- Pinch of fine sea salt
- Several grinds of black pepper
- 3 tablespoons extra virgin olive oil
- ¼ cup pomegranate seeds (optional)

Unbeatable Red Beets and Walnuts

🌿 *Makes about 5 cups (625 g); 8 to 10 servings*

I could eat beets three meals a day. I like them raw, roasted, steamed, braised, stewed, pickled, and pureed. Here I've opted for the pureeing, after simmering them gently with lots of herbs. Then I combine them with plenty of walnuts, garlic, and cilantro to give this salad its true Middle Eastern personality.

I serve this in very small bowls or espresso cups as a refreshing appetizer or as a first-course salad, accompanied by several romaine or other crisp lettuce leaves tucked around the edges, which can be used to scoop up and eat the beet salad.

TO COOK THE BEETS:

2 pounds (1 kg) beets, well-rinsed, unpeeled

4 celery stalks, strings removed, cut into 2-inch (5-cm) lengths

3 garlic cloves, minced

2 teaspoons coarse sea salt

1 small bunch of flat-leaf parsley

1 bunch of cilantro

TO FINISH THE SALAD:

2 cups (200 g) walnuts, lightly toasted

Mounded ¼ teaspoon freshly ground coriander, or to taste

3 garlic cloves, minced

2 tablespoons best-quality red-wine vinegar

Note: *Depending on the acidity of your vinegar, you may want to add a bit more than is called for in the recipe, for the dish should be a good balance of sweet and tart.*

1. To cook the beets, place them, the celery, and 3 garlic cloves in a medium, heavy bottomed saucepan. Add the coarse salt, the parsley, and the bunch of cilantro and cover with 2 inches (5 cm) of water. Bring the water to a boil over medium-high heat, then reduce the heat to medium so the water is boiling gently and cook until the beets are tender through, about 1 hour. Remove from the heat and let cool slightly. Remove the beets from the liquid and let cool. Strain the liquid and discard the vegetables and herbs. Reserve ½ cup (125 ml) of the cooking liquid.

2. While the beets are cooking, place the walnuts in a food processor and pulse several times to chop the nuts until they are finely ground but haven't gotten oily. Transfer the nuts to a large bowl.

1 cup (7 g) cilantro leaves, gently
packed

Fine sea salt and freshly ground
white pepper

3. When the beets are cool enough to handle, peel, cut them into quarters, and place them in a food processor. Add the reserved cooking liquid and pulse until they are coarsely chopped. Transfer the beets to the bowl with the ground walnuts and add the ground coriander, the minced garlic, and the vinegar. Fold the ingredients together.

4. Mince the cilantro leaves and stir into the beet mixture until all the ingredients are thoroughly combined. Add sea salt and white pepper for seasoning. Serve either at room temperature or chilled.

Malloreddus de Kita Santa—Tiny Sardinian Gnocchi for Good Friday

🌿 *Makes 4 servings*

Efisio Farris, chef and owner of Arcodoro restaurants in Dallas and Houston, Texas, "loaned" me this recipe from his native Sardinia. It is a simple, meatless pasta dish that honors the fasting of Good Friday, the leanness of the season, and the joy of herbs and nuts that punctuate all of Sardinian cuisine. Like Efisio, it bursts with personality, popping with flavor all over the mouth. Though this is an Easter season dish, I make it year-round, for it is satisfying, simple, delicious, and not your ordinary pasta dish.

   This recipe is adapted from Efisio's Book *Sweet Myrtle and Bitter Honey: The Mediterranean Flavors of Sardinia* (Rizzoli International Publications, 2007).

¼ cup (60 ml) extra virgin olive oil

3 garlic cloves, finely chopped

½ cup (5 g) basil leaves

1 tablespoon fresh rosemary leaves

½ cup (5 g) flat-leaf parsley leaves

⅓ cup (35 g) walnuts, chopped

2 tablespoons (30 g) unsalted butter, at room temperature

1 pound (500 g) malloreddus or other pasta, such as penne or fusilli

2 tablespoons fine dry bread crumbs

1 ounce (30 g) pecorino or Parmigiano-Reggiano, finely grated (½ cup)

Note: *The addition of a bit of butter here smooths out the sauce, adding a hint of luxury.*

1. Place 2 tablespoons of the olive oil and the garlic in a nonstick skillet over medium heat and cook, stirring frequently, until the garlic is softened and beginning to turn golden, about 8 minutes. Transfer the olive oil and garlic to a bowl large enough to accommodate all the pasta.

2. Mince the basil, the rosemary, and the parsley and add them, along with the walnuts and the remaining 2 tablespoons olive oil, to the garlic and olive oil in the bowl, stirring until combined. Add the butter and reserve.

3. Bring a large pot of salted water to a boil, add the pasta, and cook until it is al dente, 7 to 9 minutes. Drain the pasta, add it to the herb and oil mixture in the bowl, and toss very well, until everything is thoroughly combined and the butter is melted. Add the bread crumbs and toss, then add the cheese and toss well. Season to taste and serve immediately.

Grilled Vegetable Tarts with Pumpkin Seeds

These tarts burst with color and texture, and will delight with their combination of grilled vegetables; flaky, tender pastry; and exotic flavors. They're a perfect first course or a satisfying main course along with a big salad. You can assemble them as much as an hour before guests arrive.

1 recipe Parmigiano-Reggiano Pastry (page 236)

3 tablespoons extra virgin olive oil

2 large (10-ounce/300 g) eggplant, trimmed and cut into ½-inch (1.25-cm) thick rounds

2 medium (7-ounce/210-g) zucchini, trimmed and cut lengthwise into ½-inch (1.25-cm) thick slices

Fine sea salt and freshly ground black pepper

2 medium (9-ounce/270 g) red bell peppers

1 medium (5-ounce/150 g) onion, cut into eighths

1 tablespoon ras el hanout, or to taste

½ teaspoon sherry vinegar

Note: *Ras el hanout is a Moroccan spice mixture found easily in a Middle Eastern grocery shop. You can substitute an excellent curry powder or a dash of cumin.*

1. Line two baking sheets with parchment paper. Roll out the pastry so that it is about ⅛ inch thick. Cut out six 4-inch (10-cm) rounds of pastry and transfer them to the prepared baking sheets. Prick them all over with the tines of a fork and refrigerate until ready to bake. Save any extra pastry for another use.

2. Preheat the oven to 450°F (230°C).

3. Brush two baking sheets with 1 tablespoon of the olive oil and place the rounds of eggplant and the strips of zucchini on the baking sheet. Brush the rounds of eggplant and the zucchini with another tablespoon of the oil. Season the eggplant and zucchini lightly with salt and pepper. Place the bell peppers on a sheet of thick aluminum foil. Place the vegetables in the oven and roast until the eggplant and zucchini are golden on the bottom, 8 to 10 minutes. Flip the eggplant and zucchini, season them lightly with salt and pepper, and roast until golden

2 rounded tablespoons pumpkin
    seeds, lightly toasted

Fresh basil or chervil leaves for
    garnish

on the other side, 8 to 10 minutes longer. Remove them from the oven. Leave the peppers in the oven until they are soft and their skin is wrinkled, another 20 to 25 minutes. Remove the peppers from the oven and wrap them in the aluminium foil.

4. As soon as the zucchini is cool, dice the strips and place them in a medium bowl. As soon as the peppers are cool enough to handle, remove all the skin and seeds and dice the peppers. Add them to the zucchini in the bowl.

5. Place the remaining tablespoon of olive oil and the onion in a heavy skillet over medium heat and sauté the onion until tender through, 5 to 8 minutes. Remove from the heat and add to the vegetables in the bowl. Sprinkle 2 teaspoons of the ras el hanout over the vegetables and fold them together until all the vegetables are thoroughly combined. Taste for seasoning and add the remaining ras el hanout and salt and pepper to taste. Fold in the vinegar. Keep warm.

6. Reduce the oven temperature to 425°F (220° C). Bake the pastry in the center of the oven until the rounds are golden and crisp, about 15 minutes. Remove from the oven and transfer one to each of six warmed plates.

7. Fold the toasted pumpkin seeds into the vegetable mixture. Top each pastry with an equal number of eggplant rounds, then top the eggplant with an equal amount of the roasted vegetables. Garnish with the fresh herbs and serve.

Pistachio Music

The moon has risen full, softly illuminating the inky sky above a pistachio orchard near Aleppo, in Syria. The silvery branches of the trees shimmer like skin through wide and velvety green leaves. Hanging from them are endless grapelike clusters of nuts, their dusty-rose skins soft in the moonlight. The nuts are secretive; they give neither juice nor aroma to hint at their ripeness; the harvest moon reveals their progress.

The farmer stands at the edge of the orchard, waiting. He thinks tonight the bright green nuts may grow that final bit to burst the shell and skin. His head, bathed by moonlight, inclines. In the dark, a tiny puff of air floats through the orchard, audible to itself. Then there is another and another as nut follows nut with its final spurt of growth, bursting its shell, until all through the orchard the tiny hot breaths become music. Out under the moon more and more farmers come to hear pistachio music, the hauntingly joyful tune of the harvest.

Mushroom and Walnut Tarte Tatin

🌸 *Makes one 9-inch (23-cm) tart; 4 to 6 servings*

This is a savory play on France's most popular dessert, tarte Tatin, which is made with slowly caramelized apples baked under a tender crust. When removed from the oven, the tart is flipped onto a platter so that the caramelized apples that were hidden under the pastry now glisten in the light. This savory mushroom and walnut version, inspired by my dear friend Patricia Wells, gets the same treatment, resulting in a perfect first course for an elegant meal or a main course accompanied by a green salad.

Note: *When choosing cultivated mushrooms, look for those that are slightly open near the head of the stem; they are more mature than those that are tightly closed and will offer more flavor. Note too, that during wild-mushroom season, you can substitute any mushrooms, including cèpes, chanterelles, or morels.*

When you flip the tart and remove the pan, great care must be taken not to be burned by the steam issuing from the pan.

1. Preheat the oven to 425°F (220°C). Heavily oil a 9-inch (22.5-cm) tarte Tatin pan or a heavy ovenproof skillet.

2. Roll out the pastry on a lightly floured surface into an 11-inch (28-cm) round. Place the round on a parchment paper–lined baking sheet and refrigerate for at least 30 minutes and up to several hours. The pastry can also be frozen at this point.

3. Heat the goose fat in a 12-inch (30-cm) nonstick skillet over moderate heat until hot but not smoking. Add the mushrooms, season lightly with salt, and sauté just until they wilt and begin to give up their juices, about 5 minutes.

One-half recipe On Rue Tatin's Tender Tart Pastry (page 237)

3 tablespoons goose or duck fat or extra virgin olive oil

1½ pounds (625 g) cultivated or wild mushrooms, trimmed and cut into thick slices

Sea salt

1 cup (10 g) flat-leaf parsley leaves, gently packed

1 teaspoon fresh thyme leaves

3 garlic cloves, minced

½ cup (50 g) walnut pieces, lightly toasted and minced

Freshly ground white pepper to taste

FOR THE WALNUT OIL VINAIGRETTE:

1 tablespoon fresh lemon juice

4. Mince half the parsley.

5. Reduce the heat and add the thyme, garlic, the minced parsley, and half of the minced walnuts. Cook, stirring regularly and shaking the pan, until the mushrooms have reabsorbed most of their juices, a minute or two more. Season generously with salt and pepper and remove from the heat.

6. Transfer the mushroom mixture to the tart pan or skillet. Place the filled pan on a baking sheet. Remove the pastry from the refrigerator and place it on top of the mushroom mixture, gently pushing the edges of the pastry down around the edge of the pan. Return to the oven and bake until the pastry is golden, 20 to 25 minutes.

7. While the tart is baking, prepare the vinaigrette: In a small bowl, combine the lemon juice and salt and whisk to dissolve the salt. Add the walnut oil and whisk to combine. Taste for seasoning.

8. Remove the tart from the oven. Immediately place a serving platter with a lip atop the skillet. Quickly but carefully flip the skillet so that platter is on the bottom. Using a spatula or an offset knife, lift the skillet off the platter and let the burst of steam float away, then remove the skillet from the platter. If any mushrooms stick to the pan, gently transfer them to the top of the pastry.

9. Mince the remaining parsley and sprinkle atop the mushrooms with the remaining walnuts. Drizzle with the walnut oil vinaigrette, season with fleur de sel, and serve.

Fine sea salt to taste

¼ cup (60 ml) walnut oil, preferably Leblanc brand

Fleur de sel for garnish

Tomato and Pistachio Croustillant

Elegant. Easy. Delicious. Who could ask for anything more? Use very ripe, sweet tomatoes for this and a drizzle of pistachio oil.

Note: *Croustillant means "crisp" in French, and the pastry is very crisp, almost like puff pastry.*

I recommend assembling these at least 30 minutes and up to an hour before you plan to serve them, so the pastry and the topping have a chance to meld.

One recipe On Rue Tatin's Tender Tart Pastry (page 237)

8 ripe medium tomatoes, sliced ½ inch (1.25 cm) thick

3 tablespoons (45 ml) olive oil

Sea salt and freshly ground black pepper

6 small sprigs rosemary

10 sprigs thyme

2 sprigs summer savory or rosemary

About 4 teaspoons pistachio oil

¼ cup (about 30 g) salted pistachios, coarsely chopped

1. On a flat work surface, roll out the pastry to a ⅛-inch (.3 cm) thickness. Working quickly, cut out eight 5-inch (13-cm) circles from the pastry, transfer them to baking sheets, and chill for 1 hour.

2. Preheat the oven to 350°F (175°C).

3. Arrange the tomato slices on the bottom of two nonreactive baking dishes. Drizzle the olive oil over the tomatoes, sprinkle generously with salt and pepper, and arrange the fresh herbs on top.

4. Bake the tomatoes in the bottom third of the oven until slightly golden on top and caramelized, about 1 hour. Remove and let cool for at least 10 minutes before proceeding. Remove and discard the herbs.

5. Increase the oven temperature to 425°F (220°C).

6. Remove the pastry circles from the refrigerator and prick them several times with a fork. Bake in the oven until light brown, 18 to 20 minutes. Remove from the oven and let cool to room temperature on wire racks.

7. Assemble the croustillants by arranging three slices of tomato overlapping slightly in the center of each pastry round. Let sit for about 30 minutes and up to 1 hour. Just before serving, drizzle each croustillant with $1/2$ to 1 teaspoon of pistachio oil and sprinkle with an equal amount of pistachio nuts.

Fiona's Almond and Olive Sandwich

🍀 *Makes 4 servings*

When my daughter, Fiona, doesn't have school on Saturday morning, she and I can be found pursuing a well-trodden path through our farmers' market. One of our stops is at Makram's stall. Makram is a big, burly Tunisian, with a smile like the sun and velvet brown eyes. He is what the French call a *baratineur*—what some might call a "bluffer." He hails me like long-lost family, clasps his hands, and looks to heaven when he sees Fiona. All of his customers are made to feel they have caused the sun, moon, and stars to come out and shine for Makram. The response is, of course, big sales of all his products, from olives to taramasalata.

Makram is smooth and obvious, but both Fiona and I play right along with his game. Makram delights in Fiona's clear blue eyes and listens to every word she says to him. When she told him about the sandwich she makes with his herbed cheese and almond-stuffed olives, he laughed out loud and then asked her exactly how to make it. As she explained, he made one, with all his long line of customers looking on. When he was finished, he wrapped it in a napkin and handed it over the counter to her, with a flourish. "For you, my Fiona," he said.

Note: *You can adapt Makram and Fiona's sandwich by adding sun-dried tomatoes, lots of freshly ground black pepper, fresh lettuce, thin-sliced cucumber, and freshly sliced seasonal tomatoes. You may also want to vary the herbs, though a good herbes de Provence mixture is hard to beat. Note, too, that there are dozens of varieties of green olives. Makram's are Tunisian, fleshy and firm, and marinated in a salty brine.*

9 ounces (250 g) very soft fresh goat cheese

1 tablespoon extra virgin olive oil

1 teaspoon herbes de Provence

One 9-ounce (250-g) baguette, sliced lengthwise almost in half, so that when you open it it remains attached along one side

4 ounces (110 g) green olives, cut in half and pitted

1. Place the cheese, the olive oil, and the herbes de Provence in a medium bowl and mix. Taste to be sure you've added enough herbs for your taste.

2. Thickly spread each side of the baguette with the cheese, using all of it. Arrange the olives on one side of the sandwich, the almonds on the other, pressing them firmly into the cheese so they'll stay there as you eat the sandwich. Firmly press the halves of the bread back together, then cut it into four lengths on the bias. Serve with a big green salad alongside.

¼ cup (40 g) raw almonds, coarsely chopped

Almond Soup

🌿 *Makes 6 to 8 servings*

This gorgeous soup is the culinary "La Marcha Real" of southern Spain, where it is a cornerstone of the cuisine. Smooth and luxurious, it tastes distinctly of the almonds; the olive oil and garlic are a foil. The result is a combination of the elegant and the exotic. Though its origins are simple, it is a soup for all occasions.

Note: *The texture of this soup has a great deal to do with the type of bread you use. Best is a rustic-textured baguette style. The original recipe called for the soup to be passed through a sieve, but I don't strain it because I like the subtle texture of the ground almonds.*

One of the beauties of this soup is that you can make it the day before you plan to serve it. Before serving, adjust the texture by adding water a tablespoon at a time, if necessary, then carefully season it. Don't cut the garnish grapes until right before you plan to serve the soup, as they will darken.

This soup is best made in the autumn, when grapes are flavorful and garlic still has a bright freshness to it.

1. Place the bread in a medium bowl and just cover it with water. Let it sit for about 30 minutes, or until it is soft through. To drain the bread, pick it up by small handfuls and place it in the palm of one hand. Cover with the palm of your other hand so your hands are cupped, and squeeze very gently, slowly, and firmly, so that you squeeze out the water without mashing the bread, allowing the bread to retain its integrity. The bread should be just slightly moist.

¼ pound (110 g) firmly textured day-old bread

3 new or very fresh garlic cloves or 2 mature garlic cloves, peeled

1 cup (140 g) Marcona almonds, skinned

½ cup (125 ml) extra virgin olive oil

2 ounces (60 g) seedless green grapes

¼ cup (60 ml) crème fraîche

2 to 3 teaspoons sherry vinegar, or to taste

Fine sea salt and freshly ground white pepper

FOR THE GARNISH:

4 to 6 teaspoons extra virgin olive oil

6 to 8 seedless green grapes, cut in half

6 to 8 Marcona almonds, skinned, lightly toasted, and cut in half horizontally

2. In a food processor, puree the garlic, the almonds, and ¼ cup (60 ml) of the olive oil. Add the grapes, the drained bread, the crème frâiche, and about 1 cup (250 ml) filtered water, enough to make a smooth puree about the consistency of heavy cream.

3. If desired, transfer the mixture to a sieve or tamis and strain it through. Season the soup to taste with sherry vinegar, salt, and white pepper. Chill, covered, for at least 2 hours before serving.

4. To serve, adjust the seasoning and the texture of the soup (by adding a bit of water if necessary), then transfer the soup to shallow soup bowls. Garnish each bowl with a drizzle of olive oil, two grape halves, and two almond halves.

Focaccia with Onions and Almonds

🍀 *Makes 6 servings*

During the two years that I researched and wrote *Italian Farmhouse Cookbook*, I discovered the simplicity of focaccia, the satisfying pizzalike bread that incorporates just enough olive oil in the dough to make it almost meltingly tender. Focaccia is forgiving because you can push the rising time a bit, add just about any ingredient, and season it as you like. Even at the best of times it is quick to make, so it can be a nearly last-minute addition to any meal. The crunch of almonds on this version with the onions and rosemary makes for a fun and intriguing flavor combination.

Note: *The dough for this focaccia should be soft and sticky as you work it. As you knead and shape it, dust it lightly with flour so it doesn't stick to your hands. The moisture in the dough makes for a light crust*

I call for "very warm" water because I use SAF instant yeast, which requires water that is warmer than usually called for in yeast breads to activate it. Use the temperature of water that works best with your yeast.

The focaccia will emerge from the oven blistering hot, so wait a while before slicing and eating it—10 minutes at least.

1. To make the dough, place 2 cups (500 ml) very warm water in a large bowl or the bowl of an electric mixer. Add the yeast, stir, then add 1 cup of the flour and stir. Let sit until the yeast bubbles up on the surface of the mixture.

2. With the mixer running, or as you stir, add the olive oil and salt and mix well. Slowly add the remaining flour, 1 cup at a time, until you have a soft dough. Coarsely chop 2 tablespoons rosemary, then stir it into the dough.

FOR THE DOUGH:

2 teaspoons SAF instant yeast

4 to 4½ cups (580 g–650 g) unbleached all-purpose flour

¼ cup (60 ml) extra virgin olive oil

1 tablespoon fine sea salt

2 tablespoons fresh rosemary leaves

FOR THE TOPPING:

3 medium (4-ounce/120 g) onions, very thinly sliced

¼ cup (60 ml) extra virgin olive oil

2 tablespoons fresh rosemary leaves

½ cup (80 g) raw almonds, coarsely chopped

Coarse sea salt and freshly ground black pepper

Beat the dough—it will be too soft to knead—until it is elastic, about 5 minutes by hand, about 2 minutes in a mixer. Cover the bowl and let the dough sit until it doubles in bulk, about 1 hour.

3. Preheat the oven to 375°F (190°C). Sprinkle an 18×13-inch (45×33-cm) baking sheet with an even layer of semolina flour or cornmeal.

4. Turn out the dough onto a heavily floured surface and, keeping the surface of the dough floured, punch down the dough several times, kneading out the air as much as you can. The dough will be quite sticky; you can handle it easily if you keep a light film of flour on it at all times. Stretch out the dough into a small rectangle. Transfer the dough to the baking sheet and stretch and push it out to a rectangle that comes to within 1 inch (2.5 cm) of the edges of the baking sheet. Let the dough rest while you prepare the topping.

5. Place the onions in a large bowl, drizzle with 2 tablespoons of the olive oil, and toss until the onions are coated with the oil. Evenly sprinkle the onions on top of the dough.

6. Coarsely chop 2 tablespoons rosemary and sprinkle it evenly over the onions, then sprinkle the almonds over all. Drizzle the remaining 2 tablespoons of olive oil over the focaccia, then season with coarse salt and black pepper. Bake in the center of the oven until the dough is golden at the edges and cooked through in the center, 35 to 40 minutes. Remove from the oven, let cool for 5 to 10 minutes, then cut into serving pieces or serve whole.

Yeast Seed Crackers

🌿 *Makes about 40 crackers*

An ideal lunch for me is a piece of buttery Comté or Montferrat cheese, a fresh endive and garlic salad, and these nutty, crisp crackers. I was inspired to make them by Lena Sodergren, a Swedish friend who makes these regularly. These are the Swedish alternative to bread, eaten with nearly every meal.

Note: *As I tried this recipe over and over, I found that some of the crackers baked to a deep gold, some to a light gold, some very, very crisp, some not so crisp. The variables had to do with how thin I rolled them out and the temperature of my oven. In Sweden, crackers are available very dark and crisp, medium-dark and crisp, or pale and pliable, so all the variations are successes.*

The nutritious omega-3 fat in flax seeds becomes more nutritionally accessible when the grains are ground, so I grind some and use the other grains whole, because I love the hit of nutty flavor I get when I bite into a seed. To grind flax seeds, put them in a food processor or a coffee grinder reserved for grinding grains.

The Swedes have a special rolling pin for these crackers. It looks quilted and has sharp points on it so that as it rolls the dough—very, very thin—it makes holes in it and gives the crackers a sort of quilted look. This keeps them flat during baking.

1 teaspoon SAF instant yeast

1 cup (145 g) whole wheat flour

1 scant tablespoon coarse sea salt

1 cup (130 g) rye flour

3 cups (435 g) unbleached all-purpose flour

2 tablespoons toasted sesame oil

6 tablespoons Dukkah (page 50)

2 tablespoons poppy seeds

1 tablespoon ground flax seeds

1 tablespoon whole flax seeds

1. Place 2 cups (500 ml) very warm water in a large bowl or the bowl of an electric mixer. Add the yeast and ¼ cup of the whole wheat flour, stir, and let sit until the yeast foams on top of the water. Add the remaining whole wheat flour and stir, then add the salt and stir. With the machine running, or as you stir, add the rye flour, then add 1 cup of the all-purpose flour and mix well. Let the mixture sit in a warm spot until it bubbles and doubles in volume, about 1 hour.

2. Add another $1/2$ cup of the all-purpose flour to the dough and mix well, then stir in the sesame oil. When it is thoroughly incorporated, add the dukkah and the seeds and mix well. Add enough of the remaining all-purpose flour to make a fairly firm dough, and when the dough is too firm to stir in the machine or by hand, turn it out onto a heavily floured surface and knead in enough flour so that the dough doesn't stick to your hands, flouring the work surface and the dough regularly as you knead. You will probably use a total of 2 to $2\frac{1}{2}$ cups of all-purpose flour to achieve this. When the dough is kneaded, place it back in the bowl and cover it with a damp towel. Leave it to rise in a warm spot (68° to 70°F/20° to 21°C) until it has nearly doubled in bulk.

3. Preheat the oven to 400°F (200°C). Dust several baking sheets with flour or semolina.

4. Punch down the dough. Cut it into 8 pieces. Roll out each piece on a lightly floured surface, making sure to flour the top of the dough as well so the rolling pin doesn't stick to it, until it is paper-thin and about 8 inches in diameter. Cut each piece into the shape and size of cracker you want. Transfer the crackers to the prepared baking sheets. The crackers can be right next to each other, but they shouldn't be touching.

5. Poke each cracker several times with the tines of a fork to make holes for the steam to escape as they bake. Let the crackers rise for about 15 minutes, just long enough that the gluten in them relaxes slightly, then bake them in the center of the oven until they are golden on the bottom, about 12 minutes. Turn the crackers and continue to bake them until they are crisp and golden on both sides, 5 to 8 minutes longer, or as long as you like to achieve the cracker you prefer.

6. Turn off the oven, open the oven door, and leave the crackers in the oven to dry thoroughly, up to 2 hours. Remove the crackers from the oven and transfer them to cooling racks. Serve or store in an airtight container when completely cool for up to 1 month.

Salads

Salads

A salad is one of the best reflections of the season's bounty. In this collection of recipes, each season is represented, from winter through autumn. Winter salads are composed of greens with earthier flavors, like escarole and curly endive, whereas spring and summer salads are lighter and include flowers and more tender greens such as butter and oak leaf lettuce and young arugula. Nuts make these salads special and extraordinarily tasty and healthful as they add their flavors, textures, and considerable health benefits.

Serve these salads as a beginning or an end to a meal or even as a light main course.

En avant—let's go—for the season's best!

Millet with Saffron and Walnuts

🌸 *Makes 4 to 6 servings*

Millet, an ancient, toothsome grain, was considered sacred in China as far back as 4000 B.C., where it was eaten and fermented into wine. In India, millet was used to make flatbread thousands of years ago, and millet grew with pistachios and other plants in the hanging gardens of Babylon. There are many varieties of millet—supposedly even crabgrass is a relative, and teff, the grain used to make the fluffy Ethiopian bread called *injera,* is another variety.

Millet has a delicate flavor, making it a perfect backdrop for spices, herbs, and walnuts, as here. This is ideal as a vegetarian main course, or it can be served alongside steamed or grilled meat or fish. Take it along on a picnic, too, for a tasty change. This is lovely with a lightly chilled Beaujolais.

Note: *Toasting the millet brings out its flavor. A plus to this tiny grain is that it contains no gluten and can be substituted in any recipe calling for rice.*

1 cup (200 g) millet

½ teaspoon saffron threads, crushed using a mortar and pestle

2 fresh bay leaves or dried imported bay leaves

1 6-inch-long rosemary branch

1 large bunch of chives

½ cup (5 g) cilantro leaves

½ cup (50 g) walnuts, toasted and finely chopped

Fine sea salt

½ cup (125 ml) yogurt

1. In a large skillet over high heat, toast the millet until it begins to pop, 1 to 2 minutes. Transfer the millet to a medium saucepan. Add 2½ cups (625 ml) water, the saffron, bay leaves, and rosemary, and bring to a boil, covered. Decrease the heat to medium-low and cook, covered, until the liquid is absorbed, about 30 minutes. Remove from the heat and let cool to room temperature.

2. Mince the chives and the cilantro.

3. Place the millet in a medium bowl and fluff it with a fork. Stir in the cilantro, chives, and walnuts. Season with salt to taste, remove the bay leaves and rosemary branch, and serve, with the yogurt alongside.

Watercress and Beet Salad with Almonds

🌿 *Makes 6 servings*

This salad bounces around the palate the way winter sun bounces off snow. It is bright and vivid in both color and flavor, and every time I serve it, murmurs of delight fill the room. Serve this during winter and into spring, when watercress is fleshy and green, and beets are filled with deep sugar.

Generous ½ cup (95 g) almonds, lightly toasted, or 24 green almonds

1 medium or 2 small beets

1 tablespoon balsamic vinegar

Sea salt and freshly ground black pepper

⅓ cup (80 ml) extra virgin olive oil

2 shallots, sliced paper-thin

6 cups watercress sprigs

Note: *If you can still get watercress in early summer, sprinkle the salad with the raw green almonds available then instead of mature almonds—green almonds are tender and white, and they have an elusive almond flavor and aroma. They are available from www.green almonds.com. This salad with its deep green and lusty dark red colors is also great for Christmas dinner.*

Serve a lightly chilled white wine such as a Gaillac from Domaine Peyres Roses.

1. Coarsely chop the toasted almonds. Or, if using raw, green almonds, crack the outer shell and peel off the inner golden skin to reveal the tender young almond. Reserve.

2. Bring 3 cups water to a boil in the bottom of a steamer. Add the beets to the steamer and steam until they are tender through, 30 to 40 minutes. When the beets are cool enough to handle, peel and cut them into small dice. Reserve.

3. In a large bowl, whisk the vinegar with salt and pepper to taste until the salt dissolves. Slowly whisk in the olive oil until the mixture is emulsified. Stir in the shallots and season to taste.

4. Place 2 tablespoons of the dressing in a small bowl. Add the diced beet and toss so all the pieces are coated thoroughly with dressing. Reserve.

5. Add the watercress to the remaining dressing in the large bowl, toss gently but thoroughly so the watercress leaves are coated with the dressing, and then add the almonds. Toss again and divide among six plates, making sure the almonds are arranged so they can be seen. Sprinkle equal amounts of the beets atop the salad and serve immediately.

Edgy Greens with Roquefort and Hazelnuts

🍂 *Makes 6 servings*

Johanne Killeen and George Germon of Al Forno and Tini restaurants in Providence, Rhode Island, have a lively interest in food and life, which shows in this robust and satisfying salad. What makes this salad special is the combination of intense flavors and textures, from the creamy saltiness of the Roquefort to the nuttiness of toasted hazelnuts echoed in the hazelnut oil, and finally the cacophony of flavors from the edgy greens and endive.

I use the term *edgy greens* instead of *bitter greens* because calling greens bitter isn't really fair. The word *bitter* is off-putting. In fact, "bitter" greens are those with taste—and a certain edge.

This salad calls for a Chardonnay without much oak, such as one from Domaine Mont d'Hortes.

FOR THE VINAIGRETTE:

1 tablespoon sherry vinegar

1 tablespoon balsamic vinegar

½ teaspoon fine sea salt

1 small egg yolk (optional)

1 shallot, sliced paper-thin

2 tablespoons hazelnut oil

2 tablespoons extra virgin olive oil

¼ cup (40 g) hazelnuts, lightly toasted and finely ground

Note: *The vinaigrette contains a raw egg yolk. If you prefer, you may omit this from the recipe. The vinaigrette will not be as creamy without it, but it will be tasty.*

1. In a medium bowl, whisk together the vinegars, salt, and egg yolk if using. Whisk in the sliced shallot, then slowly add the oils, whisking constantly, until the mixture is emulsified. Whisk in the ground hazelnuts, which will further thicken the vinaigrette.

2. Place the greens and the endives in a large bowl. Add the dressing and toss thoroughly until all the leaves are

10 cups (270 g) edgy greens, such as radicchio, dandelion greens, and curly endive, washed and torn into small pieces

2 Belgian endives, trimmed and cut into thin lengthwise slices

6 ounces (180 g) Roquefort cheese, at room temperature

Freshly ground black pepper

coated. Evenly divide the salad among six salad plates. Crumble equal amounts of the Roquefort over each salad, then season generously with black pepper. Serve immediately.

Pine Nuts and Red Peppers

🌿 *Makes 4 servings*

Just the name of this dish makes me want to sit down at table, fork in hand, ready to tuck in. I love red peppers just about any way, though grilled and dressed with extra virgin olive oil is one of my favorite ways to enjoy them. Here they're dressed up with feta cheese and pine nuts, and they make a fine, satisfying first course, an accompaniment to grilled meat, fish, or poultry, a sandwich filling . . . you name it.

Serve this with a lively red wine, such as a Fronton from Château la Colombière in southwest France.

2 pounds (1 kg/4 large) red bell peppers, roasted (page 94), peeled, and seeded

2 tablespoons extra virgin olive oil

2½ ounces (75 g) feta cheese

1 cup (8 g) flat-leaf parsley leaves, gently packed

¼ cup (35 g) pine nuts, lightly toasted

Note: *Look for pine nuts from Italy, which are slender and torpedo shaped, rather than those from China, which are flat and almost triangular, as the flavor and texture of the former are far superior.*

Also, when buying feta cheese, buy it in a single piece if you can. Turkish and Greek fetas, made from sheep's milk, are the best.

There are several ways to roast a pepper; see page 94.

1. Be sure the peppers are thoroughly cleaned and there are no seeds hiding in them anywhere. Cut the flesh into ¼-inch (.6-cm) wide strips. Place the strips in a bowl, toss with 1 tablespoon of the olive oil, and reserve.

2. Place the feta into a small bowl and drizzle with the remaining tablespoon of olive oil. Gently mix the oil into the feta with your fingers or a fork, crumbling the feta as you mix, but not mashing it. Reserve.

3. Just before you plan to serve the peppers, mince the parsley, add it to the peppers, and toss until the peppers and parsley are thoroughly combined. Transfer the peppers to four salad plates. Arrange an equal amount of the feta on top of each portion, then sprinkle the pine nuts, which should be nice and golden, over all. Serve with fresh bread or crackers.

Roasted Bell Peppers

Under the Broiler:

Place the oven rack 3 inches from the broiler element. Place the peppers on a sheet of aluminum foil and broil, turning them frequently. When the skin is completely dark, after 6 to 8 minutes, remove the peppers from the oven and wrap them in the aluminum foil.

On the Stovetop:

Turn the flame to high and balance as many peppers on the burner as will fit easily. Once the skin in contact with the flame turns black, rotate the pepper. When the peppers are black all over, transfer them to a waiting paper bag, close the bag, and let the peppers cool to room temperature.

On the Grill:

Place the peppers about 1½ inches (4 cm) from the coals and turn them frequently, until they are black all over, about 5 minutes. Transfer them to a paper bag, close the bag, and let cool to room temperature.

When the peppers are cool enough to handle, remove as much skin as you can using your fingers. Then cut off or pull out the stem end, carefully so that it brings as many of the seeds with it as possible. Cut open the pepper and scrape out the remaining seeds. Trim away any white ribs from the pepper. Turn over the pepper and place it on a clean work surface. Remove any remaining black skin by scraping the pepper with a knife or using a paper towel. Avoid rinsing the peppers, which will wash away their flavor.

Butternut Squash and Arugula Salad

🍀 *Makes 6 servings*

This recipe came to me from Nancy Dow, who visited our home from Australia as part of an international goodwill organization. What I love about it is . . . well . . . everything, from the lushness of the squash and garbanzo beans (also called chickpeas) to the toasty crunch of the pumpkin seeds. It's colorful, it's lively, it's filled with good things, and most of all it tastes simply wonderful. This salad makes a substantial main-course dish for a vegetarian meal.

FOR THE VINAIGRETTE:

Zest of 1 lime, minced

3 tablespoons (45 ml) freshly squeezed lime juice

1 teaspoon freshly ground cumin

¼ teaspoon hot paprika, or to taste

2 garlic cloves, minced

Fine sea salt and freshly ground black pepper

¼ cup plus 2 tablespoons (90 ml) extra virgin olive oil

FOR THE CHICKPEAS:

1 cup (200 g) dried chickpeas (to give 2 cups cooked chickpeas)

1 teaspoon cumin seeds

¼ teaspoon baking soda

Note: *The recipe calls for butternut squash, which is luscious here, but you may substitute any winter squash except for a jack-o'-lantern-type pumpkin. Cute as they may be, they have very little flavor, and their texture is too watery to hold up.*

As you toast the seeds, quickly over medium heat, they'll pop and crackle to let you know when they're toasted through.

Note, too, that you may use canned chickpeas here; they aren't as tasty as those you'll cook, but they will do in a pinch.

1. Place the lime zest in a small bowl. Whisk in the lime juice, cumin, paprika, garlic, and salt and pepper to taste. Whisk in the olive oil. Taste for seasoning and reserve.

2. Place the chickpeas in a saucepan and cover them with 2 inches (5 cm) of water. Add ½ teaspoon of the cumin seeds and the baking soda and bring to a boil. Remove from the heat and let sit for 1 hour. Drain the chickpeas and cover them with 2 inches (5 cm) of water. Add the remaining ½ teaspoon of cumin seeds and bring to a boil over medium-high heat. Reduce the heat

1 spring onion or 3 scallions with about 2 inches (5 cm) of their green tops intact, trimmed and diced

TO COOK THE SQUASH:

3 pounds (1.5 kg) butternut squash, peeled, seeds removed and reserved, flesh cut into 1-inch (2.5-cm) cubes

2 tablespoons extra virgin olive oil

Fine sea salt and freshly ground black pepper

FOR SERVING:

1 cup (10 g) cilantro leaves, gently packed

½ cup (5 g) flat-leaf parsley leaves, gently packed

8 cups arugula leaves, torn into bite-sized pieces

¼ cup (35 g) squash seeds, lightly toasted

Fleur de sel and freshly ground black pepper (optional)

so the chickpeas are boiling gently and cook, partially covered, until the chickpeas are tender through but still somewhat crisp and have nearly doubled in size, about 40 minutes. Remove from the heat and drain, reserving the cooking liquid. Add half the lime vinaigrette to the chickpeas and toss. Add the onion or scallions and toss. Cool to room temperature.

3. Preheat the oven to 425°F (220°C). Place the squash in a bowl, toss with the 2 tablespoons of olive oil, and season generously with salt and pepper. Turn out the squash onto a baking sheet or a roasting pan and roast in the center of the oven until it is tender through, about 30 minutes. Remove from the oven and prepare the rest of the salad.

4. Mince the cilantro and the parsley leaves and whisk them with a bit of the vinaigrette.

5. To serve, toss the arugula with all but 2 tablespoons of the remaining vinaigrette and arrange the leaves on a large serving platter. Taste the chickpeas for seasoning and moisture and adjust. If they seem dry, add some of the cooking liquid, tablespoon by tablespoon, until they are moist, then spoon them atop the arugula. Place the warm squash atop the chickpeas and drizzle with the remaining 2 tablespoons of vinaigrette. Sprinkle with the seeds, season with fleur de sel and pepper, if desired, and serve.

The Perfect Salad Dressed with Nut Oil Vinaigrette

❋ *Makes 8 servings*

The first nut oil I ever had was made from fresh walnuts harvested by hand in the orchard on the Dubois farm in the Dordogne. The nuts would leave in big baskets, to return from the oil mill as golden oil, tidily packaged in bottles that were stored carefully away from light and heat, to be used throughout the year.

My friend Dany uses the oil in everything from vinaigrettes to a dressing for green beans or frying eggs for a last-minute first course. She started me on a similar course, and since those halcyon days of discovery I've tasted oil made from just about every nut and used them in a variety of dishes. Salads remain my favorite vehicle for nut oils, though, and here I give you a basic recipe. Use the nut oil, the salad greens, and the toppings of your choice and make unforgettable starters or finishes for your meals.

1½ tablespoons best-quality sherry vinegar or fresh lemon juice

1 shallot, sliced paper-thin

Sea salt and freshly ground black pepper

⅓ cup (80 ml) nut oil (walnut, hazelnut, peanut, pumpkin seed, almond, macadamia, sesame)

10 cups (9 ounces/270 g) mixed salad greens and fresh herbs, such as curly endive, escarole, dandelion greens, arugula, radicchio, thyme, small sage leaves, or lemon verbena

Note: *If using sesame oil from Japan, you will want to use half the amount and add another oil (peanut, olive, or canola) for the balance. If you are serving the salad as a first course, you'll want to add the cheese and toasted nuts. If serving the salad after the meal, you'll just want to serve the salad greens dressed in the vinaigrette.*

1. In a large salad bowl, whisk together the vinegar, shallot, and salt and pepper to taste. Slowly add the oil, whisking constantly, until the mixture has emulsified. Add the greens and toss until they are thoroughly coated with the vinaigrette. If you are serving the salad before the meal, scatter it with the toasted nuts or seeds and the cheese. If this is a postmeal salad, serve it with just the flowers.

½ cup (50 g) walnuts, almonds, peanuts, pumpkin seeds, sesame seeds, or macadamia nuts, lightly toasted and coarsely chopped (optional)

4 ounces (110 g) soft goat cheese, Roquefort, or feta cheese, crumbled (optional)

5 to 6 freshly picked blossoms, including nasturtiums, pansies, thyme flowers, rose petals, geranium petals

Portrait of a Nut Oil Mill

The buttery aroma of hazelnuts wafts up from the crisp green salad on the plate, yet there isn't a nut to be seen. The salad is that exquisite French creation, a mélange of tender-fresh lettuce leaves dressed lightly in a tangy vinaigrette. Yet that hazelnut aroma is devilishly palpable. Where, oh where, is it coming from?

Jean-Charles Leblanc, from the village of Iguérande in Burgundy, turns out to be the sorcerer behind the aroma of hazelnuts in the salad I am enjoying. He is head of a family enterprise called l'Huilerie Artisanale J. Leblanc et Fils, which supplies France and beyond with the world's finest nut oils. The oils, which come from just about every nut in the world, including the rare argan nut from Morocco, make their way into more than just salads. I've had the Leblanc almond oil drizzled over a tender fish fillet, the walnut oil in a moist cake, the pine nut oil perfuming a bowl of pasta, and the pistachio oil seasoning a plate of avocado and grapefruit.

The Leblancs aren't the only nut oil producers in France. There are too many to count, since nearly every region that produces nuts claims small mills that produce oil for local consumption. But the Leblancs' oils are something special.

Jean-Charles follows in the footsteps of his great-grandfather, who started the mill in 1878. Then local farmers brought their walnuts and rapeseed to the mill.

The mill still sits in the family barn at the

edge of the D982 road, which runs right through Iguérande, a wide spot on this southern Burgundian road. Anne Leblanc, Jean-Charles's sister, who grew up in the house next to the barn and now runs the family shop in Paris, describes Iguérande as *paumé*, or "lost, nowhere." But nowhere has become somewhere because of the family oil mill.

While en route to a recent visit, the minute I turned onto the D982 I knew I'd arrived, for the air smelled of toasting nuts. I walked into the Leblanc boutique and was greeted warmly by Mme. Leblanc, Jean-Charles's mother. She called her other son, Jean-Michel, the accountant and communications director for the company, and within minutes we were standing in the heart of the oil mill.

Daniel Demours, one of the company's two employees who aren't family members, scooped the coarsely crushed nuts into a blackened pot that sat over a gas flame. "We cook the nuts to add flavor and allow the oil to separate," Jean-Michel said. Mr. Demours checked the cooking nuts every few minutes. "These are pine nuts, and they cook quickly," he said as he opened the lid and deftly stirred the mash, which had already turned from solid to almost liquid in the heat. "Most of the nuts cook for about twenty minutes, but you've got to watch these carefully; they take about five."

He walked over to the presses and checked the flow of oil coming from them. It was pine nut oil, and the trickle was thin, signaling that the presses were ready for more. He ran to the pot, removed the lid and inhaled, then tipped the runny mass into a container. "The nuts are cooked. That's what we do here really—cooking," he said with a nod.

He opened a press and removed the flat disks of compressed, nearly dry nut paste left after the oil is extracted. Each was separated by a woven mat, which filters the oil.

He poured some cooked pine nuts into the press, covered it with a filter, poured in more nuts, and continued until the press was nearly full. Then he cinched it closed, put a barrel under the spigot, and waited for the golden liquid to flow into a waiting barrel.

Once a barrel is filled, it sits in the cool barn for a period of days to allow the oil to decant. The oil is then bottled, labeled, and stocked in a warehouse behind the mill. "I say it's stocked," Jean-Michel said with a laugh. "We don't really have any stock, because we sell all we produce as quickly as we produce it."

Just then a farmer and his wife walked into the barn with a sack of walnuts. Jean-Charles weighed it on an old scale. "This is the last of this year's harvest," the farmer said. "I bring them in when I need more oil." The couple left with a gallon jug of oil.

The Leblancs now get only one-third of their walnuts locally, with the rest coming from nearby Périgord. As for the other nuts that go into more than a dozen varieties of oils they produce, their provenance reads like a map of the world. Hazelnuts from Italy and Turkey, pine nuts from China (those from Italy don't give as much oil), almonds and pecans from California, pistachios from Iran, poppy and squash seeds from Austria, peanuts from the southern United States.

The Leblanc oil mill produces about 300 liters (quarts) of oil per day, 365 days a year. The elder Mr. Leblanc, Jean-Charles and Jean-Michel's father, who is eighty-two, still delivers to clients within a fifty-mile radius. One of these is Franck Lesaige, chef and owner of Le Relais St. Julien in nearby St. Julien de Jonzy.

"I use the Leblanc primarily in first courses," said Mr. Lesaige. "One of my favorites now is a Royale de Foie Gras. I dress quarters of artichoke heart in pistachio oil, balsamic vinegar, shallots, and chives, then top it all with a foie gras cream." He adds hazelnut oil to *tête de veau*, or boiled head/cheese, and generally slips nut oils in whenever he has the inspiration.

Like that hazelnut oil on my salad, the Leblanc oils permeate the culinary culture of France and beyond, making it a warmer, toastier, more flavorful place.

Main Courses

Shrimp Biryani with Cashews

Nutty Mussels

Spiced Mackerel in Parchment with Pine Nuts

Fish Fillets Stuffed with Dill, Pine Nuts, and Parsley

Marinated Fish with Sesame and Macadamias

Gingered Fish on Spiced Macadamia Butter

Brazil Nut Fish

Hanger Steak with Horseradish and Walnuts

Lamb Shoulder with Apricots and Walnuts

Pistachio- and Pepper-Stuffed Lamb Fillet

Lamb and Apples with Pistachios

Roast Pork with Pistachios and Dried Apricots

Duck Breast with Almonds, Garlic, and Cumin

Chicken with Walnuts and Pomegranate Molasses

Tagine from Le Casbah

Sicilian Sweet and Sour Rabbit

Tofu Satay

Main Courses

Main courses offer so much ground for creativity and experimentation. The dishes in this chapter offer more than just gorgeous flavor and texture. They offer new ideas and the promise of many wonderful meals.

The biggest surprise in this chapter may be the abundance of seafood and nut dishes. I discovered this near-holy association when I worked on the *Great American Seafood Cookbook* and have been pursuing it ever since. Why do seafood and nuts complement each other to such a satisfying degree? I think it is a subtle contrast between lean and rich, tender and crunchy, toasty and smooth. And there is always the element of surprise to consider as well, for combining mussels, for example, with toasted hazelnuts doesn't automatically come to mind. Try it once, however, and you'll be addicted.

As good as seafood is with nuts, so are meat and poultry. Lamb is particularly felicitous with nuts, but beef is wonderful, and so are veal and pork. And of course there is poultry, which goes with everything.

Note: When buying fish, make sure it is firm and sweet smelling and looks appetizing. Never buy any fish or seafood that smells fishy or of ammonia. If you cannot find the quality or variety of fish you are looking for, get something that looks better or wait to buy fish another day, when the selection is up to your standards.

When buying shellfish, look at it carefully—it should look fresh and smell fresh. Shrimp is fine when frozen—to thaw it, leave it in the refrigerator overnight or, in a pinch, run it under cold water.

If your recipe calls for a fillet, try to get one with the skin on, as it holds the meat together during cooking. Cut across the fillet to make the individual servings or ask your fish merchant to do this for you. If you can find only skinless fillets, use them and transfer the fish carefully from cook pot to plate. Be sure to let cooked fish rest for at least 5 minutes before dressing a platter or plate. As it rests it will give up watery juices, which should be drained away since they contain little flavor and will dilute any sauce or condiment added to the fish.

When you buy poultry, insist on quality, just as you do for all the rest of your ingredients. Try to buy organic poultry directly from the person who raised it. If you cannot, be discerning in the best way you can. Be careful of labels with words like *natural* or *free range*, which don't mean an awful lot. As an example, the official definition for *free-range poultry* is that the poultry must be "allowed access" to the out-of-doors, and "access" can be the presence of a window in a barn or hangar. The same goes for meat—if you can, buy directly from the producer.

And now, as we say in France, *"À vos fourchettes!"* ("To your forks!")

Shrimp Biryani with Cashews

🌿 *Makes 6 servings*

Traditionally, each element of this Indian dish is prepared separately, then layered in a dish and baked in the oven. I have taken the liberty of deconstructing it and omitting the baking step because I want you to appreciate the individual flavors and the way each contributes to the harmony of the whole. It's also easier. The cashews are primordial to this dish, adding a contrasting toasty crunch and their characteristic smooth butteryness. Try this with a dry Riesling.

FOR THE RICE:

1½ cups (260 g) basmati rice

1 tablespoon (15 g) unsalted clarified butter (see page 108)

¼ teaspoon saffron threads

2 teaspoons fine sea salt

FOR THE TOPPING:

3 tablespoons (45 g) unsalted clarified butter (see page 108)

1 medium onion, very thinly sliced

½ cup (70 g) raw cashews

1 tablespoon raisins

Fine sea salt

FOR THE SHRIMP:

4 garlic cloves, peeled

One 1-inch (2.5-cm) piece fresh ginger, peeled

Note: *Garam masala is a spice mixture that is the foundation of much Indian cooking. A basic garam masala contains cumin, peppercorns, ginger, cardamom, cloves, cinnamon, coriander seeds, and bay leaves. If you don't have any among your spices, you can either make it or do as I do and add the individual spices as you go.*

If using frozen shrimp, place them in the refrigerator the night before you plan to use them, in a strainer set over a bowl, to give them a chance to thaw at least partially and rid themselves of any coating of ice they may have. If you don't have time to do this, give the shrimp a quick rinse under cool water, place them in a tea towel, and rub them to remove the ice coating. Otherwise the dish will be watery. The recipe calls for 1 pound (500 g) medium shrimp, which will give you 31 to 35 individual shrimp. You may add or subtract from that amount as you wish.

Don't omit the salt when you pound the garlic, ginger, and chile; it creates some friction and helps any liquids emerge from the ingredients.

1. Rinse the rice under cold running water until the water runs nearly clear. Place the rice in a small bowl,

One 1-inch (2.5 cm) chile such as Thai pepper or jalapeño, seeded

Pinch of salt

2 tablespoons unsalted clarified butter (see page 108)

1 pound (450 g) onions, very thinly sliced

⅓ cup (3 g) mint leaves, firmly packed

½ cup (5 g) cilantro leaves, loosely packed

1 tablespoon fennel seeds, crushed

1 teaspoon curry powder, preferably Madras

½ teaspoon coriander seeds, crushed

½ teaspoon freshly ground cumin

½ teaspoon ground cinnamon

⅛ teaspoon freshly ground cloves

Seeds from 5 cardamom pods, crushed, or about 20 black seeds

1 tablespoon freshly squeezed lemon juice

Fine sea salt

1 pound (500 g) fresh or frozen medium shrimp, peeled, deveined if necessary (see Note on shrimp)

cover it with water, and soak for 30 minutes. Let it drain for 30 minutes before cooking.

2. Once the rice has drained, heat 1 tablespoon of clarified butter in a medium, heavy skillet over medium heat. Add the saffron and cook just until it begins to send its aroma into the air, about 1 minute. Add the rice and cook, stirring constantly, until it looks translucent, about 2 minutes. Add 3 cups (750 ml) boiling water and the 2 teaspoons fine sea salt. Cover and cook until the rice is fluffy, about 20 minutes. Remove from the heat. The rice will stay warm for at least 40 minutes with the lid kept on the pan.

3. While the rice is cooking, make the topping. Place a sieve over a heatproof bowl. Heat the 3 tablespoons of clarified butter in a heavy pan over medium heat. Add the onion and cook, stirring and shaking the pan often, until the onion turns dark golden, 10 to 12 minutes. Add the cashews and raisins and sauté until the cashews are golden and the raisins are plump, 3 to 4 minutes. Season generously with salt, mix well, then transfer the topping to the sieve and reserve.

4. Place the garlic, ginger, and chile in a mortar or a small food processor with a pinch of salt and either crush or process to a rough paste. Reserve.

5. Melt the final 2 tablespoons clarified butter in a large, heavy skillet over medium heat. When the butter has melted but before it is blistering hot, add the onions and cook, covered, stirring occasionally, until they soften and begin to turn golden at the edges, about 8 minutes.

Freshly ground black pepper

Cilantro and mint sprigs for
    garnish

6. Mince the mint and the cilantro leaves.

7. Stir in the garlic and ginger paste and cook, stirring, until the aroma of the paste fills the air, about 2 minutes. Add the spices and the minced mint and cilantro leaves and cook, stirring gently, until the spices send up their aromas and are golden, 1 to 2 minutes. Stir in the lemon juice, then pour on ¾ cup (185 ml) hot water and ½ teaspoon salt. Stir and cook the onions until they are softened and half the water has evaporated, about 7 minutes. Add the shrimp to the onions, stir until they are coated with the onions and spices, and cook, stirring occasionally, just until the shrimp turn pink and curl, 5 to 8 minutes. Taste for seasoning and remove from the heat. Don't be concerned if the shrimp aren't cooked through; they will continue to cook in residual heat and will be cooked by the time they are served. Season to taste with salt and pepper.

8. To serve, place the steaming rice on a large serving platter and make a well or a trough in the center of the rice. Top the rice with the shrimp and onion mixture. Garnish with the reserved topping and several of the fresh herb sprigs. Serve immediately. The result is a dish of vivid liveliness, one that will cheer you up if you're down or take you a notch higher if you're not!

Note: *There are several ways to clarify butter: a quick method is to take cultured, organic butter and put it in a pan over medium-high heat. When the butter melts and begins to boil, let it boil for about 4 minutes, then remove from the heat. When the butter has cooled, skim off any foam from the top. Carefully pour off the beautiful golden liquid you find in the pan, being careful to leave behind all the milk solids that have settled in the bottom of the pan.*

Nutty Mussels

🌸 *Makes 4 servings*

At Parisian restaurant 21 Mazarine, chef Paul Minchili, a genius with fish and shellfish, combines flavors and textures that show seafood at its best. This dish is inspired by one he serves at the restaurant, which I have whenever I go. It is so heady with flavor I can never resist!

As the mussels open from the steam of their own juices, the hazelnuts, along with the other ingredients, settle inside the shell so that each mouthful is a burst of flavor and texture. I serve these either as a small first course or as a larger portion for a main dish, accompanied by plenty of fresh bread.

Note: *There is no need to remove the hazelnut skins in this recipe, as the entire nut, with skin, adds flavor and texture. You do need to remove from the mussels the beard, or byssus, which is like a string the mussel uses to attach itself to something solid. It must be removed right before the mussel is cooked, but not in advance or the mussel will spoil. You may be able to find "cleaned" mussels. These have had their byssus cut off, so there is no need to pull it out.*

- 4 pounds (2 kg) mussels, shells washed
- 1 tablespoon fresh rosemary leaves
- 3 tablespoons extra virgin olive oil
- ⅓ cup (50 g) hazelnuts, diced
- 1 small fennel bulb (about 1½ ounces/45 g), diced (⅓ cup)
- 1 thick coin fresh ginger, peeled and minced (½ teaspoon)
- 2 tablespoons freshly squeezed lemon juice
- 2 tablespoons dry bread crumbs
- Freshly ground pepper

1. If necessary, debeard the mussels right before you begin to prepare the dish. Keep them in the refrigerator.

2. Mince the fresh rosemary, and cover to keep the aroma from dissipating.

3. Heat the olive oil in a wok over medium heat. Add the hazelnuts and cook, stirring constantly, until they begin to turn golden and smell toasty, about 7 minutes. Increase the heat to medium-high. Remove the hazelnuts from the pan. Add the fennel and ginger to the pan and cook, stirring frequently, until the fennel is tender, about 4 minutes. Stir in the lemon juice, then add the mussels to the wok. Sauté them, stirring them almost constantly, until they open and most but not all of their juices have evaporated, about 7 minutes. Return the hazelnuts to the pan along with the bread crumbs and continue stirring and sautéing until the mussels are cooked through and the bread crumbs are mixed throughout and beginning to smell toasty, about 3 additional minutes.

4. Stir in the minced rosemary and remove the mussels from the heat. Season them with pepper to taste and serve immediately.

Spiced Mackerel in Parchment with Pine Nuts

🌸 *Makes 4 servings*

Many people claim not to like mackerel, the taste of which is often described as "strong." When they try it prepared this way, however, cooked in its own juices, delicately swaddled in parchment, seasoned with sweet spices, then topped with toasty pine nuts, their minds are changed and opinions completely reversed.

Note: *When choosing mackerel, look for very firm fish that smells sweet and of the sea. Mackerel has a more intense smell than other fish, but it should always be appealing. Check each fillet for bones and remove them by making what is called a V cut. Place the blade of your very sharp knife alongside the row of bones, holding it at a 45-degree angle, and cut right to the skin, but not through it. Repeat on the other side and pull out the slim strip of flesh that contains the bones. The fillet will remain intact.*

Eight medium (about 2 ounces/60 g each) mackerel fillets, bones removed

2 tablespoons pine nuts

1/4 teaspoon black peppercorns

4 cloves

1/2 teaspoon ground cinnamon

Generous pinch of piment d'Espelette or hot paprika

Fine sea salt

3/4 teaspoon dried oregano

Fleur de sel

Fresh oregano sprigs for garnish (optional)

1. Preheat the oven to 450°F (230°C).

2. Rinse the fillets and pat them dry. Refrigerate until just before cooking.

3. Place the pine nuts in a small, heavy skillet over medium heat and toast them, shaking the pan often so the nuts toast evenly, until the nuts are golden, 4 to 5 minutes. Transfer the pine nuts to a bowl and reserve.

4. Grind the pepper and the cloves to a fine powder in a spice grinder or coffee grinder reserved for that purpose

and mix in a small bowl with the cinnamon and piment d'Espelette. Lightly season each fillet with salt, then sprinkle an equal amount of ground spices evenly over each fillet. Sprinkle each fillet with an equal amount of dried oregano.

5. Cut four 12×8-inch (30×20-cm) sheets of parchment paper. Fold horizontally in half, then unfold them. Lay two seasoned fillets on each piece of parchment paper, about 2 inches (5 cm) below the fold line. Fold the upper half down over the fish so the edges meet. Brush the edges with water, then make a narrow fold all the way around to form a pocket, pressing firmly on the fold. Make another fold, this time crimping the edge as you go to seal the packet well. Repeat with the remaining fillets and either refrigerate until you are ready to bake them or set them on a baking sheet and bake in the preheated oven until the parchment packets are puffed and golden, about 6 minutes.

6. Remove the fillets from the oven. Cut open the packets and carefully transfer the fillets to warmed serving plates, arranging them in a X on the plate, crossing them at the tail end. Drizzle the fillets with their juices, sprinkle them lightly with fleur de sel, then sprinkle the pine nuts over and around the fillets. Garnish the plates with the oregano leaves if using and serve immediately.

Fish Fillets Stuffed with Dill, Pine Nuts, and Parsley

🍀 *Makes 4 servings*

The preferred fish for this Swedish recipe is herring, but where I live in Normandy, herring is available for a very short period. Since I like to make this dish year-round, I use mackerel. If you cannot find either fish, use trout fillets, preferably organically farm-raised or wild.

Note: *When transferring the cooked fish to the plate, first transfer the fillet with the stuffing on top of it, then top it with the other fillet. Some of the filling will tumble off the fillet, creating a garnish on the plate.*

1. Rinse the fillets and check them carefully for bones. Remove any bones. Pat them dry and refrigerate.

2. To make the stuffing, heat 1 tablespoon of the olive oil in a small skillet over medium heat and sauté the pine nuts and the garlic, stirring and shaking the pan often so they brown evenly, until both are golden, about 7 minutes. Remove from the heat and reserve.

3. Mince the herbs and stir them into the pine nuts and garlic, along with the lemon zest and 1 teaspoon of the remaining oil. Reserve.

4. Heat the remaining tablespoon of oil in a very large nonstick skillet over medium heat or divide the oil between two skillets. When it is hot but not smoking, place the fillets in it, skin side down. Season them with salt and pepper. Evenly divide the stuffing atop four of the

8 small (3 ounces/90 g each) herring, mackerel, or trout fillets, skin on, bones removed

FOR THE STUFFING:

2 tablespoons plus 1 teaspoon extra virgin olive oil

¼ cup (35 g) pine nuts

2 garlic cloves, minced

¾ cup fresh dill fronds, gently packed

¾ cup flat-leaf parsley leaves, gently packed

Zest of 1 lemon, minced

Fine sea salt and freshly ground black pepper

fillets, pressing it gently onto them. Cook the fillets, covered, until they are translucent, 4 to 6 minutes. Remove the pan from the heat. Transfer each fillet with stuffing to a warmed serving plate. Generously season them with pepper. Top each with an unstuffed fillet and serve immediately.

Marinated Fish with Sesame and Macadamias

🌿 *Makes 6 servings*

This is a simple preparation that will seduce the palates of all who taste it, for who can resist toasted coconut and the buttery crunch of toasted macadamias?

While the macadamia is native to Queensland, it was introduced to Hawaii in 1851 as both an ornamental tree and one that would help reforest islands. It was only a matter of years before Hawaii became the largest producer of macadamias in the world. When I spent time in the Hawaiian islands, which are now the world's second-largest producer of macadamias, I found the nuts used ubiquitously in inspired fish dishes like this one. A white burgundy would be lovely here—try one from Domaine Mont d'Hortes.

Note: *If the exact fish you are looking for doesn't measure up to your quality standards, simply substitute another.*

The fish here can be marinated from 30 minutes to overnight. The flavor naturally intensifies the longer it marinates. Remember to turn the fish from time to time.

1. Whisk the tamari, palm sugar, shallot, and sake together in a small bowl. Rinse the fish and pat it dry, then lay the fillets in a shallow nonreactive dish and pour the marinade over them. Turn them, cover, and refrigerate for at least 30 minutes and up to 8 hours.

2. Just before serving, place the spinach in a large Dutch oven or saucepan over medium heat. Cover and cook the spinach, turning it once, until it is wilted but still bright green, 8 to 10 minutes. Remove from the heat

FOR THE FISH AND THE MARINADE:

- 1½ tablespoons tamari or soy sauce

- 1 tablespoon palm or light brown sugar

- 1 shallot, sliced paper-thin

- 1 tablespoon sake

- 1¼ pounds (560 g) firm white fish, such as lingcod, flounder, haddock, or halibut, bones and skin removed, cut into 6 equal pieces

- About 6 firm lettuce leaves, such a those from a head of escarole or romaine

and transfer the spinach to a colander to drain. When the spinach has cooled enough to handle, press on it to remove as much liquid as possible—there should still be a slight bit remaining in the spinach, so that it isn't completely dry. Coarsely chop the spinach, transfer it to a medium bowl, and drizzle it with the soy sauce and sesame oil. Toss thoroughly, taste for seasoning, then reserve, keeping the spinach warm.

3. Bring 3 cups (750 ml) water to a boil in the bottom half of a steamer. Line the top of the steamer with the lettuce leaves. When the water is boiling, place the fish in the steamer and cook until it is opaque through, about 7 minutes. Transfer the fish from the steamer to a platter and cover it loosely with aluminum foil to keep it warm.

4. To serve, reheat the spinach if necessary, then divide it evenly among four warmed dinner plates, patting it gently into a small round in the center of the plate. Cover the spinach with a piece of fish, then sprinkle each serving with 2 tablespoons of the macadamia sprinkle and serve.

FOR THE SPINACH:

1 pound (500 g) spinach, trimmed and rinsed, with the water still clinging to it

1 tablespoon tamari or soy sauce

1/2 teaspoon toasted sesame oil

FOR THE GARNISH:

1/2 cup (125 ml) Macadamia and Coconut Sprinkle (page 228)

Gingered Fish on Spiced Macadamia Butter

❧ *Makes 6 servings*

Nut butters are so versatile, and macadamia butter is one of the best. Here it is teamed with spices and citrus to provide a foil for fish. This is a dish you can make rain or shine, winter or summer, with just about any type of gorgeous fresh fish you find. The play of flavors is fresh and lively, and the resulting dish is easy on the eye.

Note: *I prefer a lean white fish to contrast with the macadamia nut butter, but salmon or swordfish works too. Make this as spicy as you like by leaving in or removing the chile seeds. I recommend using a miniature food processor to make the sauce.*

1. Rinse the fillets and pat them dry. Check them for bones and remove any you find. Refrigerate until just before cooking.

2. To make the macadamia butter, place the nuts in a food processor and pulse until they are quite finely chopped. Add the ginger, chile, and lime zest and process until all the ingredients are finely chopped and the nuts begin to form a paste. Add the lime juice and salt and continue processing until you have a buttery paste. Transfer the paste to a small bowl and reserve.

3. To cook the fish, heat the olive oil in a large non-stick skillet over medium heat. When it is hot but not smoking, add the fillets, skin side down. Place three rounds of ginger atop each fillet, evenly spaced. Lightly season each fillet with salt and white pepper. Cover the

Six 5- to 7-ounce (180- to 210-g) white fish fillets, such as lingcod, sea robin, or flounder, with skin on

FOR THE MACADAMIA BUTTER:

¾ cup (105 g) macadamia nuts, toasted

One ¼-inch (.6-cm) coin fresh ginger, peeled and coarsely chopped

One 1-inch (2.5-cm) piece fresh chile, seeds removed if desired

Zest of 1 lime

2 tablespoons (30 ml) freshly squeezed lime juice

Generous ¼ teaspoon fine sea salt

TO COOK THE FISH:

2 teaspoons extra virgin olive oil

fillets and cook until they are opaque through, 6 to 8 minutes. Remove the pan from the heat and uncover it. Let the fillets sit in the pan while you finish preparing the plates.

4. While the fish is cooking, form a generous teaspoon of the macadamia butter into a rough pyramid. Set aside and repeat five times. Spread about 2 tablespoons of the remaining macadamia butter in the center of each of six warmed dinner plates, roughly spreading it out the same size as the fillet.

5. To serve, remove and reserve the three slices of ginger atop each fillet. Lay a fillet atop the macadamia nut butter spread on the plate, skin side up. Place a pyramid of the macadamia nut butter next to the fillet and arrange three of the cooked ginger slices next to the fillet, overlapping them slightly. Their edges will be curled, and they will look like a flower set next to the fish. Arrange three cilantro leaves on each plate so they look attractive. Season the fish lightly with fleur de sel. Repeat with all of the plates and serve immediately.

One 1½-inch (4-cm) piece fresh ginger, unpeeled, cut into 18 paper-thin slices

Fine sea salt and freshly ground white pepper

18 fresh cilantro leaves

Fleur de sel

Brazil Nut Fish

🍀 *Makes 4 servings*

I almost feel as if I should apologize to Brazil nuts. Since childhood I had avoided them in favor of cashews, pistachios . . . just about any other nut. Now that I've written this book, I have a great appreciation and taste for them.

While I don't snack on Brazil nuts—it's not really a great idea to do that since they are high in selenium, and health care professionals recommend eating no more than six at one sitting, I love cooking with them. Aside from their exotic upbringing—they're harvested by hand in the rain forest, they refuse to be cultivated, they have their own special bee to pollinate them—Brazil nuts have a dense texture and an intriguing flavor. Here they make this crisp fish extraordinary.

I like to serve steamed vegetables such as broccoli, cauliflower, potatoes, sweet potatoes, turnips, even fennel with poppy seed dressing (see dressing recipe page 232) alongside this dish.

1. Using a mortar and pestle or in a small food processor, grind the nuts with the salt until they are quite fine, just before the powder stage. If there are a few larger pieces of nut, that's fine. Stir in the flour and paprika, then transfer the mixture to a shallow dish or plate.

2. In a small bowl, whisk together the egg and 1 teaspoon water until thoroughly combined and slightly foamy. Transfer the egg mixture to a shallow dish.

3. Place the oil in a large skillet and heat it over medium heat.

8 whole Brazil nuts, lightly toasted and coarsely chopped

½ teaspoon fine sea salt

¼ cup plus 2 tablespoons (55 g) unbleached all-purpose flour

½ teaspoon paprika (half hot, half sweet if you like)

1 egg

2 to 3 tablespoons mild cooking oil, preferably grapeseed

1 pound (450 g) firm white fish fillets, such as cod, lingcod, or tilapia, bones removed, cut into 4 serving pieces

4. Dip each piece of fish into the egg mixture, then into the nut and flour mixture. Pat the nut mixture all over the fish if it doesn't stick evenly, so it is covered evenly.

5. When the oil is hot but not smoking, place the fish in the pan and cook until it is golden on each side and translucent in the center, 7 to 10 minutes total. Serve immediately.

Hanger Steak with Horseradish and Walnuts

🍀 *Makes 6 servings*

Hanger steak seasoned with creamy horseradish and melted onions emerges from its quick roasting crisp on the outside, tender and juicy inside, and infused with the flavor of the golden walnut and horseradish stuffing. The cooking juices are simple and hearty and make a lovely drizzle atop the meat. Try serving this with the Nutty Fresh Shell Beans (page 164) or Brussels Sprouts and Potatoes with Poppy Seed Dressing (page 167) and a Côteaux du Languedoc, such as Musardises from Domaine les Grands Costes.

Note: *Hanger steak—a long, thin, lusciously flavored and textured piece of beef—is called* onglet *in French. The roasting time is short, so that the meat remains rare. If you prefer your beef more well done, roast as directed and let it rest for a longer time. If you prefer more of a horseradish bite, use regular horseradish rather than creamy.*

1. For the stuffing, place the olive oil and the onions in a medium skillet over medium heat and stir. Cook the onions until they are translucent through and soft, about 10 minutes, stirring frequently so they don't turn golden. Season to taste with salt and pepper, remove from the heat, and cool.

2. Mince the parsley.

3. In a small bowl, mix the parsley, horseradish, and walnuts. Taste for seasoning and adjust.

FOR THE STUFFING:

2 tablespoons extra virgin olive oil

2 medium red onions, diced

Fine sea salt and freshly ground black pepper

½ cup (5 g) flat-leaf parsley leaves

⅓ cup (80 ml) creamy-style horseradish

¼ cup (25 g) walnuts, lightly toasted and minced

1 pound (500 g) hanger steak

1 cup (250 ml) robust red wine, such as a Cabernet Franc from the Languedoc

½ cup (125 ml) stock or water

4. Cut the hanger steak crosswise into two equal portions, then slice down the center of each steak but not all the way through it (butterfly), so that you can open the steaks like a book. Spread one-third of the horseradish mixture inside each steak. Place one-third of the cooked onions atop the horseradish mixture in each hanger steak and season with pepper. Close the steaks over the filling as though you were closing a book, pushing any onions inside the steak if they threaten to ooze out.

5. Spread the remaining third of the horseradish on top of one of the hangar steaks, season it with salt and pepper, and top it with the remaining onions. Set the other hangar steak on top, pressing the two firmly together. Tie the steaks together with kitchen string to create what looks like a beef roast.

6. Preheat the oven to 450°F (230°C).

7. To cook the steak, place it in a roasting pan. Pour the wine and stock or water into the pan, add the bay leaves, and place the pan in the center of the oven. Roast until the steak is rare and tender to the touch, about 20 minutes, basting it twice and adding more stock or water to the pan if necessary. You don't want all the liquid to cook away. Remove the bay leaves. Transfer the meat to a cutting board and keep it warm by covering it with an aluminum foil tent.

8. To make the sauce, place the roasting pan over medium heat and bring the cooking juices to a boil. (If there aren't many juices, add ½ cup [125 ml] wine to the pan). Boil just until the juices have reduced to a light

2 fresh bay leaves from the *Laurus nobilis* or dried imported bay leaves

2 tablespoons (30 g) unsalted butter, cut into 4 small pieces, chilled

Lovage or celery leaves for garnish

Fleur de sel

syrup. Correct the seasoning, and whisk in the butter. Strain the sauce into a pitcher or a bowl.

9. Remove the strings from the steak and cut it into 1/2-inch (1.25-cm) thick slices. The slices may fall apart, but you'll see that you can arrange them nicely on the plate.

10. To serve, place three lovage or celery leaves in the center of each of six warmed plates. Arrange two slices of beef atop the leaves, then drizzle the slices with the reduced cooking juices. Season with fleur de sel and serve with any remaining juices on the side.

Laurus Nobilis

Laurus nobilis is the botanical name for the tree that gives the delicately perfumed bay leaves that go into so many stews, soups, sauces, and other savory and sweet dishes. Native to southern Europe, the Lauris nobilis *gives us the Turkish bay leaf so often called for in recipes. It shouldn't be confused nor eschewed in favor of the California bay,* Umbellularia californica.

Lamb Shoulder with Apricots and Walnuts

🌿 *Makes 8 to 10 servings*

Lamb is, hands down, my favorite meat, no matter what the cut. It isn't just the flavor of lamb I find pleasing, but the fact that it is so versatile. It can be seasoned or left plain, made sweet or salty, cut into chunks or left whole, grilled or braised. Its flavor and texture rise to any occasion.

Here, apricot marmalade and walnuts turn lamb shoulder into a sweet and sour masterpiece.

Try a lovely, lush Corbières with this, such as one from Clos de l'Anhel.

One 3¼-pound (1.7 kg) lamb shoulder, at room temperature

¼ cup (60 ml) apricot preserves

1 cup (100 g) walnuts, lightly toasted and finely chopped

½ teaspoon ground cinnamon

Coarse sea salt and freshly ground black pepper

1 cup (250 ml) dry white wine

2 fresh bay leaves from the *Laurus nobilis* or dried imported bay leaves

1 large thyme sprig

One 4-inch (10-cm) rosemary sprig

Note: *Ask the butcher to remove the blade bone from the shoulder and to loosen but leave in the upper leg bone.*

The herbs in the wine that surrounds the lamb are a flavorful addition; always use fresh herbs, as their flavor is so much brighter than dried.

I suggest using cinnamon from Vietnam or Indonesia, which pretty much covers the world's major cinnamon-producing areas. I prefer Vietnamese cinnamon for its spicy, hot bite, while the Indonesian spice is a bit more mellow. The main point is to buy and use quality cinnamon. Visit www.penzeys.com.

1. Preheat the oven to 400°F (200°C).

2. If the upper leg bone hasn't been loosened, cut around it with a knife to detach the meat from it.

3. In a small bowl, mix together the preserves, walnuts, and cinnamon. Rub the mixture over the inside of the lamb shoulder, tucking a fair amount of the stuffing into the space created by loosening the meat from the bone. Season with salt and pepper. Tie the lamb into a packet with kitchen string, keeping the apricot stuffing mixture and the leg bone, if you have it, inside the packet. You will end up with a roundish packet.

4. Place the lamb in a heatproof nonreactive baking dish and pour the wine around it. Place the herbs in the wine and roast until the lamb is browned on the outside, resists slightly when pressed, and has an interior temperature of about 145°F (63°C) for medium-rare, about 1¼ hours, basting it occasionally with the liquids in the pan. Remove from the oven, sprinkle the shoulder with coarse salt, and transfer it to a cutting board with a trough around the edge, to catch any juices that emerge from it. Cover the lamb with a tent of aluminum foil and let it sit for at least 20 minutes and up to 40 minutes, to allow the juices to be reabsorbed.

5. Place the baking dish over medium heat and bring the cooking juices to a gentle boil. Remove the herbs and reduce the cooking juices until they are the consistency of a thin syrup. Taste for seasoning.

6. To serve, remove the string from around the lamb and slice it into ¼-inch slices. Drizzle with the cooking juices and serve.

Pistachio- and Pepper-Stuffed Lamb Fillet

🌿 *Makes 4 servings*

I spent an unforgettable evening in the kitchen with Fatih Babacon, chef of the restaurant Mahana in Gaziantep, Turkey, watching him prepare his very special version of traditional Antep Turkish dishes. He uses the best possible ingredients and stays close to tradition. Here, a tender piece of lamb is flattened and rolled around a moist and flavorful stuffing of dark red pepper paste, leeks, yogurt, and pistachios, then quickly grilled over a wood fire. This would be perfect with a Côtes de Provence from Clos d'Alari.

1 tablespoon plus 1 teaspoon extra virgin olive oil

2 large leeks, trimmed, rinsed well, and diced

1 garlic clove, minced

1 pound 6 ounces (680 g) lamb fillet

1 tablespoon tomato paste

1 teaspoon Turkish pepper paste

2 tablespoons whole-milk Greek-style yogurt

Sea salt and freshly ground black pepper

⅓ cup (55 g) pistachio nuts, finely chopped

Note: *I use what the French call a fillet of lamb, from the neck. In North America, it is best to use a fillet from the lamb round or upper thigh. Pound it gently to flatten it, but don't use too much force; meat is best if its cellular structure remains intact. If you cannot find the deep, rich Turkish pepper paste (biber salcasi, available by mail order from kalustyans.com), use an extra teaspoon of tomato paste and 1 tablespoon mild to hot paprika, or to taste. Precede this with Parsley, Green Olive, and Walnut Salad (page 63) and accompany it with Potatoes with Yogurt and Pistachios (page 160).*

1. Build a fire in the grill or fireplace. When the coals are red and dusted with ash, place the grate about 3 inches (8 cm) above the coals.

2. Place 1 tablespoon of the olive oil in a medium, heavy pan. Add the leeks and garlic and stir to coat them with the oil. Place the pan over medium heat and cook, stirring frequently, until they are tender, 5 to 7 minutes. Remove from the heat.

3. Lay out the lamb on a work surface. Butterfly it (or ask your butcher to do this) by cutting nearly all the way but not quite through the length of the piece, and spread it open. You may need to pound it slightly to flatten it; if so, pound it gently so as not to compromise the texture of the meat. Spread the meat with the tomato and pepper pastes, then with the yogurt. Top with the leek mixture, arranging it in a thin line down the length of the lamb, about 1 inch (2.5 cm) from the edge. Lightly season with salt and pepper, then sprinkle the pistachios atop the leeks. Roll the long side of the lamb back over and atop the leek and pistachio stuffing, enclosing the stuffing within it. Tie the roast firmly in several places to keep it together. Brush or rub the lamb with the remaining teaspoon of olive oil.

4. When the grate is hot, place the lamb on it, directly above the coals, and cook until the side closest to the fire is golden and crisp, about 5 minutes. Turn the roast until it is golden all over, a total of 15 to 20 minutes, depending on how rare you like lamb. Fifteen minutes results in perfectly cooked, but slightly rare, lamb.

5. Remove the lamb from the grill and let it sit for about 10 minutes. Remove the string, then slice the lamb into rounds 1½ inches (4 cm) thick. Serve immediately, drizzled with any juices that have emerged from the lamb.

A Pistachio Family

We drive on from our orchard crew, turning down a dirt road, our tires roiling up dust behind us. Suddenly a chicken darts across the road. The driver screeches to avoid it, misses, then swerves on two tires into the yard of a nondescript building where two young boys watch with wide eyes.

Kamil descends from the car to greet a wiry man with a bushy mustache who has emerged from the building. I'm worried there will be a confrontation, and I see worry on Kamil's face too, but the men greet each other like old friends and are immediately laughing together. Kamil pokes his head into the car. "He tells me a chicken is a chicken," he says, as relieved as I am that there will be no retribution in this distant outpost.

The man, Mustafa Oguler, is chief of the tribe that lives in this area. Kamil doesn't know him well, although he's worked with him for nearly two years to improve the productivity of the tribe's pistachio orchards. Mr. Oguler ushers us into the building, which is a large room with beautiful carpets on the floor, and matching pillows lining the walls. We are joined by his brother Lahti, and within minutes of our taking our seats on the pillows, the older of the boys returns enveloped in the aroma of the mint tea he carries in along with bowls of pistachio nuts. These he sets on the floor in the center of the room, then he pours everyone a glass of the sweet, heady tea and settles near his father to watch and listen. We are less than an hour from the urban center of Gaziantep, yet it feels as if we've traversed centuries.

The men talk pistachios, farming, and family, which represent, I think, the universe of this place. The conversation is punctuated by cracks of pistachio shells. I listen for a long while, occasionally asking a question, and then finally broach the subject of local cooking. An abrupt silence falls. It is as if I've entered forbidden territory as I ask about food, favorite dishes, important ingredients, who does the cooking and where. The men look at one another, converse, look at me, then converse some more, and pretty soon Kamil says, "They will take you to meet their wives."

We walk from our room, which I've learned is the tribal reception area, through the new-fallen darkness to a large bungalow behind it. Kamil and I are left on our own for a few minutes, then we are joined by the chief and his brother, their wives and mother, and a large handful of children. It's quite an audience, the atmosphere exceedingly friendly, warm, and lively as all those people with their range of eyes from nearly black to ice blue to pale green look from us back to one another as they whisper and giggle loudly.

I ask about cooking, and the chief's wife turns to her mother, they laugh, then she says, "It's a big job; we are usually at least eighteen at table for meals."

The children continue to stare as they jiggle, climb over and around one another, then finally fall silent. We are, apparently, fascinating. I'm busy asking questions, which Kamil is gamely translating, but it's rough going. His English, though excellent, doesn't include culinary vocabulary or the names of any ingredients. We talk, we hesitate, I ask about favorite dishes, everyone is smiling, and smiling, and smiling. Finally the chief's wife approaches and takes my hand, pulling me gently to follow her. We go around the back of the house to a sort of shed that contains a countertop and a hole in the floor over which is set a big pot. This is the stove. A stack of *eckmeck*, freshly baked bread that is brushed with a mix of flour and water before it goes into the oven in the corner, sits on the counter. All the heat in this kitchen comes from wood.

I learn that the dishes issuing most regularly from this rudimentary kitchen are lamb stews with fruits or vegetables of the season; stuffed bulgur dumplings; salads of cucumber and tomatoes; hummus topped with boiling olive oil; chicken with pistachios; bulgur and yogurt soup. The women and children crowd into this utensil-less, potless, accoutrementless kitchen as they hasten to explain what they make.

I signal to Kamil that we must leave. He translates, and faces fall. They want us, expect us, to share a meal. I'm heartbroken. There is nothing I would love more, but I'm expected at an official dinner in the city, one I must attend. There is much conversation, much head shaking, many appeals, and then finally the chief's wife asks Kamil to take a picture. "Of all us hardworking women," she says, including herself, her sister, her mother, and me. She embraces me, hard, and we stand with our arms around each other.

"You'll eat with us next time, and you'll help me cook," she said, her smile wide. "I need the help!"

I tell her I look forward to it, and I mean it. As we drive away I feel warmed by the welcome of this tribal family.

Back in Gaziantep I am ushered into a large and stately apartment and introduced to a small group of urbane residents of Gaziantep, including the mayor. I am taken into the kitchen to see dozens of dishes in mid-preparation, then back out to the dining room to chat politely through the apéritif hour. When dinner is ready, we go to the dining table, which is now laden with what I saw being prepared in the kitchen.

There is lamb with apples, stuffed bulgur dumplings, a beautiful olive and parsley salad (page 63), orange flower water and pistachio wheat starch pudding, gorgeous clear jellies with candied fruits and nuts floating in them, and more. I wasn't the only one exclaiming over the food's goodness and beauty, its abundance and skilled preparation.

As I eat this exquisite food, each bite truly is better than the one before it, I think about where I had been in the afternoon. That spot where I'd stood and embraced a shrouded woman felt like an entirely different world from this one. Yet it was the same country, the same culture. When the common thread is food and cuisine, distances seem so very, very short.

Lamb and Apples with Pistachios

🍀 *Makes 6 servings*

A true classic of Antep cooking, from the east Anatolian area of Turkey, this dish is easy to identify for the classic bright green pistachios and rich-tasting dried pepper paste (available at Middle Eastern markets or at kalustyans.com), tender lamb, and a host of spices. All combined, the ingredients evoke a "wow" when the dish is served, for it is unusual, bright, satisfyingly delicious. I owe this dish to Mrs. Sermin Ocak, the recognized master chef of Gaziantep, Turkey, who served this to me as part of a sumptuous meal she prepared for a group of her friends.

This would be lovely with a white Burgundy.

Note: *This is traditionally made with quince, but because they are hard to find, I adapted the recipe for apples. By all means, use quince if you have them. If using apples, try a firm variety such as Cox Orange Pippin, Fuji, or Pink Lady. The garnish of apple slices may seem tricky or fussy, but the slices atop this dish are beautiful against the lamb and the green of the pistachios. The apple garnish fits just as well if you've used quince in the recipe.*

2 tablespoons extra virgin olive oil

1¾ pounds (860 g) boneless lamb shoulder, cut into 1½-inch (4-cm) cubes

Fine sea salt

1½ pounds (675 g) white onions, cut into eighths

1 tablespoon Turkish pepper paste (biber salcasi)

¼ cup (60 ml) tomato paste

½ teaspoon freshly ground allspice

4 medium (about 3 ounces/90 g each) firm, tart apples or quince, peeled, cored, and cut into 1½-inch (4-cm) cubes

⅓ cup (55 g) pistachios, lightly toasted

1. Place the olive oil in a large, heavy saucepan over medium-high heat and add the lamb. Season it lightly with salt and brown it on all sides, about 8 minutes. Remove the lamb from the pan, reduce the heat to medium, and add the onions. Cook, stirring often, until the onions are golden and softened, about 10 minutes. If the onions are sticking, add 1 or 2 tablespoons of water to the pan.

2. While the onions are cooking, whisk together ½ cup (125 ml) filtered water, the pepper paste, and the tomato paste.

3. Return the lamb to the pan with the onions and the tomato paste and pepper paste mixture. Add the allspice, some salt, and the apples and stir well, scraping up any browned juices from the bottom of the pan. Bring the liquid to a boil, reduce the heat so it is simmering merrily, cover, and cook, stirring occasionally, until the lamb and apples are tender through, about 1½ hours. Check occasionally to be sure there is enough liquid in the pan that the meat and onions aren't sticking and add a bit more if necessary.

4. When the meat is tender, remove it from the heat. Taste for seasoning. At this point you may let this dish sit for several hours and then reheat it. It will just become more flavorful as it sits. If, once you are ready to serve it, it is soupy, increase the heat to medium-high and reduce the cooking juices until they are slightly thickened.

5. About 5 minutes before serving, stir the pistachios into the dish. Set the apple slices for the garnish in the dish, laying them atop it, cover the dish, and let it sit for 5 minutes. The slices will steam just slightly in that time and absorb a bit of flavor from the sauce.

6. To serve, carefully remove the apple slices and set them aside. Evenly divide the dish among six shallow soup bowls. Delicately arrange the apple slices atop each serving, so the colorful skin shows. Season with fleur de sel if desired and serve.

1 small, firm, moderately tart apple, preferably with very red skin, cored, skin on, very thinly sliced, for garnish

Fleur de sel (optional)

Roast Pork with Pistachios and Dried Apricots

🌼 *Makes 6 servings*

Pistachios originate in countries where pork is forbidden, yet they are often combined with pork in other cultures. In France, for instance, it is hard to find a pork pâté without the bright green of pistachio nuts studding its texture. The pistachios are added primarily for their counterpoint of color, but also for their soft crunch. In this recipe, apricots are added to the mix, along with a bit of cardamom, to give the dish another layer of flavor, sweetness, and flair.

Try a Château de Roquefort Côtes de Provence (Les Genêts) with this sumptuous dish.

Note: *Try to find pork that has been raised with care, from a small, preferably organic farm.*

1. Preheat the oven to 375°F (190°C).

2. Coarsely chop all but 2 tablespoons of the pistachio nuts. Reserve the chopped pistachios. Using a small knife, poke as many shallow (½-inch/1.25-cm) holes in the pork roast as you have whole pistachios and insert the whole pistachios into the holes.

3. In a small bowl, combine the chopped pistachios, apricots, and honey until thoroughly combined. Add the cardamom, ¼ teaspoon sea salt, and several grinds of pepper and mix well. Taste and adjust the seasoning.

4. Place the pork loin on a work surface. Press it out or unroll it so that it is flat on the cutting board. If it is very

½ cup plus 2 tablespoons pistachio nuts (90 g), toasted and skinned

One 2-pound (1-kg) boneless pork loin

4 ounces (110 g) dried apricots, diced

2 tablespoons floral honey, such as lavender

½ teaspoon freshly ground cardamom

Fine sea salt

Coarsely ground pepper, preferably a blend of white, green, and black

2 tablespoons extra virgin olive oil

thick in one part, slice partway into that area and fold it out to make the piece of pork an even thickness. What you are looking for is a relatively even, flat piece of pork. Spread the filling over the meat, going to within about 1½ inches (4 cm) of the edges. Roll up the pork as you would roll a flat cake for a jelly roll, as tightly as you can, and tie it together using kitchen twine. You may need to use skewers as well to keep it in one piece.

5. Place the loin in a roasting pan. Rub it all over with the olive oil. Place the onions around the pork. Pour 2 cups (500 ml) of the wine over and around the pork, place the bay leaves in the wine, season the pork lightly with salt, and roast it in the center of the oven until it is golden on the outside and cooked through (140°F/62°C), about 1¼ hours. Check the loin occasionally as it roasts, and add the remaining wine as necessary to keep the bottom of the roasting pan very moist and prevent the onions from sticking and burning (use water if you run out of wine).

6. Remove the pork loin from the oven and transfer the pork to a cutting board with a trough to trap any juices that run from it. Let the pork loin sit for at least 20 minutes before slicing it, so the juices retreat back into the meat.

7. Place the roasting pan over medium-high heat and cook, stirring up any browned bits from the bottom of the pan, and continue cooking until the cooking juices have reduced to about ½ cup (125 ml) and the onions are very tender through, almost like a marmalade, about 10 minutes. While the juices are reducing, add any juices that drain from the pork as it sits. Taste the onions and adjust the seasonings. Remove the bay leaves.

2 pounds (1 kg) red or white onions, cut into eighths

3½ cups (875 ml) full-bodied dry white wine

2 fresh bay leaves from the *Laurus nobilis* or dried imported bay leaves

Fresh herbs sprigs, such as sage, chervil, or rosemary, for garnish

8. To serve, slice the pork into slices ¼ inch (.6 cm) thick and either arrange them on a warmed platter and garnish with the onions and the fresh herbs or arrange two slices in the center of each of six warmed dinner plates, garnish with the onions and herbs, and serve immediately.

Duck Breast with Almonds, Garlic, and Cumin

🌿 *Makes 4 servings*

Duck breast is one of the finest meats of all, and the accompaniment of toasted almonds with garlic and cumin makes for a unique combination. The almonds are chopped, then sifted before being cooked to a golden turn in the duck fat, then they are added to softened onions, spiked with a bit of cumin salt, and set off with a drizzle of reduced orange juice. The result is a dish that looks as if you spent all day making it—but you won't.

I drink a deep, rich Fronton from Château la Colombière with this.

1 cup (250 ml) freshly squeezed orange juice

¼ teaspoon balsamic vinegar

Two 13-ounce (370-g) duck breasts (magrets)

Fleur de sel and freshly ground black pepper

¾ cup (120 g) raw almonds, coarsely chopped

2 medium onions, diced

2 large or 4 small garlic cloves, cut crosswise into paper-thin slices

Mounded ¼ teaspoon Cumin Salt (page 226), or to taste

1 tablespoon unsalted butter, cut into 4 pieces, chilled

Fresh herbs for garnish

1. Place the orange juice in a medium, heavy pan over medium heat. Bring to a lively simmer and simmer until the juice is thickened to a syrup and has reduced by about two-thirds, about 10 minutes. Check the juice frequently to be sure it isn't reducing too quickly. Remove from the heat, whisk in the vinegar, and reserve.

2. Heat a heavy skillet over medium heat. When it is hot but not smoking, add the duck breasts, skin side down. Cover and cook until the skin is deep golden, about 8 minutes. Turn and cook for 30 seconds, then remove them from the pan. Drain off most of the fat, reserving 2 to 3 tablespoons, and return the duck breasts to the pan, skin side down. Continue cooking them, covered,

just until the meat is done on the outside but is still very rare inside, 5 to 6 minutes more. Remove the duck breasts from the pan and place them on a cutting board with a trough to catch any juices that run from them. Season the duck breasts with fleur de sel and pepper and let them rest for about 5 minutes.

3. Place the chopped almonds in a sieve over a bowl and shake the sieve so any tiny almond particles fall through.

4. Place 2 tablespoons of the reserved duck fat in a heavy skillet over medium heat, add the onions, and sauté until they are softened, about 8 minutes. Add the almonds and cook until they are toasty and golden, 4 to 6 minutes. Add the garlic and cumin salt and continue cooking, stirring constantly, until the garlic is golden and the cumin is fragrant, 4 to 5 minutes. Don't let the almonds burn—move the skillet off the heat if it is getting too hot. Remove from the heat, season lightly with fleur de sel, and transfer to a bowl. Reserve.

5. Using the same saucepan, place the reduced orange juice over medium heat, and when it is simmering, whisk in the butter, moving the pan on and off the heat so that the butter emulsifies into the orange juice and makes it glisten.

6. Slice the duck breasts crosswise on the bias into thin slices and keep them warm. Place about 1 tablespoon of the almond and garlic mixture in the center of each plate, then top with three or four slices of the duck breasts, overlapping them. Drizzle the slices with orange sauce. Garnish with herbs and serve immediately.

Chicken with Walnuts and Pomegranate Molasses

🌿 *Makes 6 servings*

There are so many layers of flavor here, ranging from the tangy pomegranate molasses to buttery walnuts, which thicken the sauce and give it texture, to the inherent goodness of a farm-raised chicken. This dish was inspired by the Middle East, where walnuts grow in company with pistachios and grapevines and where pomegranate trees grow wild, their fruit available for the picking.

Serve a lovely Château Turcaud with this.

Note: *When grinding walnuts in a food processor, pay careful attention so they don't become an oily mess. To avoid this, add a pinch of sea salt right at the start and keep careful watch.*

If you cannot find pomegranate molasses, available at Middle Eastern markets and some supermarkets, substitute 2 tablespoons balsamic vinegar and 1 tablespoon pomegranate juice.

While this recipe is intended for chicken, it is marvelous with guinea fowl as well.

1. Place the olive oil in a large, heavy skillet over medium-high heat. When it begins to sizzle, add the chicken and brown it well on both sides, seasoning each side with salt, about 10 minutes total. Remove the chicken from the pan, reduce the heat to medium, and add the onions. Stir and cook until they are softened and golden, about 8 minutes. Add the garlic, stir, and continue cooking until the garlic is nearly cooked and beginning to turn golden at the edges, about 5 minutes. Stir in 1 cup (250 ml) water, scraping up any caramelized pieces that may have

FOR THE CHICKEN:

3 tablespoons extra virgin olive oil

One 3-pound (1.5-kg) chicken, cut into 6 serving pieces

Fine sea salt

4 small (about 4 ounces/110 g each) onions, each cut into 10 wedges

3 garlic cloves, thinly sliced lengthwise

3 tablespoons (45 ml) pomegranate molasses

2 cups (8 ounces/200 g) walnuts, ground

FOR THE HERBS:

1 cup (10 g) mint leaves, loosely packed

stuck to the bottom of the pan, then add the chicken pieces, nestling them down among the onions. Bring the water to a lively simmer, cover, and cook the chicken until it is nearly cooked through, about 25 minutes, turning it twice as it cooks. Stir in the pomegranate molasses, add another cup (250 ml) of water, stir in the ground walnuts, and continue cooking, turning the chicken twice more, until the meat is beginning to fall from the bone and the sauce is thickened, 15 to 20 minutes.

½ cup (5 g) parsley leaves, loosely packed

1 cup (7 g) cilantro leaves, loosely packed

Generous handful of herb sprigs for garnish

2. About 10 minutes before the chicken is cooked, mince the herbs and stir them into the chicken dish. Continue cooking until the flavors of the herbs have melded with the other ingredients, about 10 minutes.

3. To serve the chicken, place one piece of chicken on each of six plates. Top with a generous serving of sauce. Garnish with the herb sprigs and serve.

Tagine from Le Casbah

🍀 *Makes 4 servings*

Cherifa, a friend of mine who is of Algerian origin, owns La Casbah, an Algerian restaurant in a town near mine called Acquigny. The chefs at La Casbah are Algerian women, clad in traditional garb, who make only the most traditional of Algerian dishes from Cherifa's recipes, including this tagine. What makes this tagine better than most is the balance of almonds and spices, as well as the apples, which are included because they are the fruit of Normandy, Cherifa's adopted home.

Tagine refers to a two-piece clay oven with a peaked lid that is pierced with a tiny hole, as well as to the stew cooked inside. The ingredients are first browned in the bottom part of the oven, which is like a large, shallow dish, over the coals. Then the top is set in place, and the mixture braises and mellows. Tagines were traditionally made with what was easily available, and in the Maghreb, as northern Africa is called, that means almonds and sesame seeds, abundant dried fruits, and poultry. Chicken is typical, but here guinea fowl is used to dress up the dish, take it uptown. However, if guinea fowl is hard to get, buy a good farm-raised chicken or a leg or shoulder of lamb.

Try a lovely Beaujolais, such as one from Moulin Blanc.

Note: *Don't forget the sesame seeds atop the dish; they add not only their toasty flavor but a healthy touch of iron too.*

3 tablespoons vegetable oil, such as canola

One 3-pound (1.5-kg) guinea hen or chicken, cut into 6 serving pieces

Fine sea salt and freshly ground white pepper

4 onions, diced

Two 4-inch (10-cm) cinnamon sticks

½ teaspoon saffron threads

1. Heat the oil in the bottom of a tagine or in a heavy skillet over medium heat. Add the guinea hen, season lightly with salt and pepper, and cook until the pieces are golden on each side, a total of about 8 minutes. Remove the guinea hen and add the onions to the pan. Cook, stirring frequently, until the onions are golden, about 8 minutes. Add 1 cup (250 ml) water to the pan and stir, then add the cinnamon sticks, the saffron, 1 teaspoon salt, ½ teaspoon pepper, the ground and fresh ginger, and the cilantro and stir to thoroughly combine. Nestle the guinea hen pieces down among the onions and bring the water to a boil. Reduce the heat so the water is simmering, and cook the guinea hen, turning it at least three times so that it is impregnated with the spices, until it is tender, about 30 minutes.

2. While the guinea hen is cooking, melt the butter in a saucepan over medium heat. Add the honey, apples, and almonds and cook, stirring often, until the apples are just tender and beginning to caramelize on all sides and the nuts are golden, about 10 minutes. Watch the apples carefully to be sure they don't burn, and reduce the heat if necessary.

3. When the apples are cooked, fold them into the pan with the guinea hen, along with the almonds and their cooking juices. Stir in the orange flower water. Cover and cook just until all the flavors meld and the apples begin to melt, about 10 minutes. Remove from the heat.

4. Remove the cinnamon sticks and the bouquet of cilantro. Adjust the seasoning, sprinkle the sesame seeds over all, and serve immediately.

1 teaspoon ground ginger

1 thick coin fresh ginger, peeled and minced (about 1 teaspoon)

1 bunch of cilantro, tied together with kitchen string

3 tablespoons (45 g) unsalted butter

¼ cup (60 ml) honey

5 good-size apples, peeled, cored, and thinly sliced

½ cup (70 g) raw almonds

3 tablespoons orange flower water

2 tablespoons sesame seeds, lightly toasted

Argan Oil

I first tasted argan oil at Arpège, Alain Passard's nearly vegetarian three-star restaurant in Paris, about ten years ago. The oil had been much in the news at that time, vaunted as the latest culinary wonder, imported directly from Morocco. Dark golden and slightly gamy tasting, it didn't make me swoon, but I have become and remain a devotee because of the people behind its production, the women of the Sousse plain in southwestern Morocco.

Fruit from the argan tree (*Argania spinosa*) has long been harvested by Berbers living on the Sousse plain, the only place the twisted, thorny tree thrives. Traditionally, goats were the handmaidens of its production, for they scramble up the trees and perch on its limbs to eat the soft fleshy fruit, expelling the pit that contains the cherished nut. Today, however, while goats still do the work on remote farms, argan fruit destined for commercial production is harvested from the tree by human workers.

The production of argan oil, which has traditionally been used in Morocco as both a condiment and a cosmetic, has always been women's work, and thus it remains. Women collect the fruit and let it dry in the sun. Once dry, the nut is separated from the fruit and cracked open using a small oval stone. Inside is the oil-rich kernel. These are roasted, then ground.

Thanks to Zoubida Charrouf, a professor in the science department at Mohammed V University in Rabat, Morocco, who has made the production of argan oil a personal mission because she realized that it sustained an important rural population, and to the government of King Mohammed VI, argan oil cooperatives have been established. With the multiple goals of creating sustainable argan forests and improving women's rights, these cooperatives allow women to work in good conditions, get decent pay, and have time to take care of their children. Other countries like Monaco contribute funds to the argan project, and UNESCO has weighed in by designating the 10,000-mile argan region as a biosphere, acknowledging the conservation and sustainable development of the argan oil industry.

If, like me, you don't love the taste of argan oil, you may like the way its considerable vitamin E and essential fatty acids soften your skin and can give it what the French call *éclat*, or "luminosity." If its nutty flavor appeals to you, then do as the Berbers do and drizzle it on raw vegetables or couscous before steaming or mix it with honey and almonds to make *amlou*, a tahinilike paste. Whatever its use, argan oil sustains on every level.

Sicilian Sweet and Sour Rabbit

🌿 *Makes 6 servings*

Many dishes in Sicily are like this one, with the poetry of the Middle East wafting through their flavors, an influence from the Saracens, who came to Sicily and left behind them everything from sweet and sour sauces and apricot trees to fancifully beautiful architecture. As in many Sicilian dishes, this sauce is thickened with almonds, which along with the currants balance the tart lemon juice.

3 tablespoons almonds, coarsely chopped

3 tablespoons currants

2 tablespoons extra virgin olive oil

One 3-pound (1.5-kg) rabbit, cut into 6 serving pieces

Fine sea salt

4 medium (4 ounces/120 g each) red onions, thinly sliced

6 fresh bay leaves from the *Laurus nobilis* or dried imported bay leaves

Freshly ground black pepper

½ cup (125 ml) fresh lemon juice

1 tablespoon plus 1 teaspoon sugar

Fresh herbs such as flat-leaf parsley, basil, sage, or fennel for garnish

Note: *Chicken is a worthy substitute in this dish. Both will cook quickly as they braise in the flavorful juices, about 30 minutes from start to finish. The many bay leaves impart a sweetness to the rabbit.*

1. Place the chopped almonds and currants in a mortar or in a food processor and crush or process them to form a chunky paste. Reserve.

2. Place the olive oil in a large, heavy saucepan or Dutch oven over medium heat. When it is hot but not smoking, add the rabbit pieces, season with salt, and brown them on each side, about 8 minutes total, salting the other side when you turn the rabbit.

3. Remove the rabbit from the pan and add the onions, stir until they are coated with the oil, cover, and cook, stirring occasionally, until the onions soften, about 8 minutes. Return the rabbit to the pan and nestle it among the onions. Add the crushed currants and almonds, bay leaves, and 1 cup (250 ml) hot water. Stir, season lightly with salt and pepper, and cook, uncovered, turning the rabbit regularly and adding up to another cup (250 ml) water so that there is always a scant inch in the pan, until the rabbit is two-thirds cooked, about 20 minutes.

4. In a small bowl, whisk together the lemon juice and sugar. Add to the rabbit in the pan, stir well, cover, and continue cooking for 10 minutes. Uncover the pan and continue to cook until the rabbit is cooked all the way through and the juices have reduced somewhat, an additional 5 minutes. Season to taste.

5. To serve, remove and discard the bay leaves from the sauce. Place a piece of rabbit in the center of each of six warmed plates and spoon an equal amount of the cooking juices, onions, currants, and almonds over each piece. Garnish each with a sprig of herbs. Serve immediately.

Tofu Satay

Makes 4 servings

This is a lovely dish, based on the Indonesian satay, or saté. It is universally popular because of the peanut sauce and a boon to vegetarian and vegan alike, for it is rich in the protein of nuts and tofu and wild with spicy flavors, along with the perfume of lime juice and the allure of cinnamon-scented rice. I like to serve this with a small bowl of hot pepper flakes alongside, for those who want more spicy kick. Serve this with a simple spinach salad, and a delicious, artisanally made beer.

2 cups (330 g) basmati rice

Fine sea salt

Two 3-inch (7.5 cm) cinnamon sticks

2 tablespoons peanut oil

1 medium onion, diced

2 cups (500 ml) chunky peanut butter, or more if needed

1 cup (250 ml) unsweetened coconut milk, or more if needed

1 tablespoon plus 1 teaspoon dark brown sugar

1 tablespoon fish sauce, preferably Thai

1 tablespoon soy sauce or tamari

1 tablespoon curry paste (try Patak's brand)

1½ teaspoons curry powder, preferably Madras

Note: *Some curry pastes and powders are spicier than others—you'll want to adjust the amount of seasonings according to those you use.*

1. Put the rice in a sieve and rinse it really, really well under cold water, until the water runs clear.

2. Put the rice in a medium saucepan with 1 quart (1 liter) water, 2 teaspoons salt, and the cinnamon sticks. Bring the water to a boil over medium-high heat. Reduce the heat to medium, so the water is still boiling, and continue cooking until there are bubble holes in the top of the rice and all the excess water has boiled away, about 10 minutes. Cover and cook for 10 minutes longer. Then remove the rice from the heat to let it sit and plump. Don't even be tempted to remove the lid; it needs to rest undisturbed for 10 minutes.

3. While the rice is cooking, make the peanut sauce. Put 2 teaspoons of the peanut oil in a small skillet with the onion. Stir to coat the onion with the oil, season lightly with salt, and cook, stirring occasionally, until the onion

146 Nuts in the Kitchen

2 limes

1½ pounds (625 g) tofu, drained
  and sliced into 3 × 2-inch
  (8 × 5-cm) slices

⅓ cup (3 g) flat-leaf parsley
  leaves

is softened but not browned, 7 to 8 minutes. Remove it from the heat and reserve.

4. Put the peanut butter into a medium saucepan. Slowly whisk in the coconut milk, brown sugar, fish sauce, soy sauce, curry paste, and ¾ teaspoon of the curry powder. Stir in the cooked onion.

5. Bring the peanut sauce just to a boil over medium-high heat. Reduce the heat to low and simmer until the sauce has thickened somewhat and the flavors meld, about 15 minutes.

6. Squeeze ½ lime into the peanut sauce, stir, then adjust the seasoning. If you'd like the sauce thicker, whisk in more peanut butter, 1 tablespoon at a time. If you'd like it thinner, whisk in coconut milk, 1 tablespoon at a time. Adjust the seasoning and keep the sauce warm over low heat.

7. Heat the remaining peanut oil in a skillet over medium-high heat. When the oil is hot, add the tofu—stand back, because it might spit. Season the tofu lightly with salt and the remaining ¾ teaspoon curry powder. Cook it, stirring constantly, until it is golden on all sides, 4 to 6 minutes. Remove from the heat and put the tofu in a shallow bowl.

8. Squeeze another ½ lime over the tofu and toss it.

9. Right before serving, mince the parsley leaves and cut the remaining lime into 4 wedges. Place the rice in a shallow serving bowl and arrange the tofu on top. Pour the peanut sauce over all, then sprinkle with the parsley and serve garnished with the lime wedges.

A World of
Side Dishes

Curried Belgian Endive with Cashews

Roasted Eggplant and Hazelnut Caviar

Quinoa with Macadamia Nuts

Butternut Squash with Leeks and Pecans

Gorgeous Green Spinach with New Garlic

Potatoes with Yogurt and Pistachios

Parsnip and Walnut Fricassee

Nutty Fresh Shell Beans

Sauteed Carrots East Indian Style

Brussels Sprouts and Potatoes with Poppy Seed Dressing

Spiced Rice with Toasty Nuts

A World of Side Dishes:
Nuts, Vegetables, and Grains

From Curried Belgian Endive with Cashews to Nutty Fresh Shell Beans, you'll find in this chapter a variety of nut-laced dishes you can use in a meal to enhance it with flavor, texture, color, and taste. I call the dishes here side dishes because they go so well alongside meats, poultry, seafood, soups, and salads. But the versatility of each means it can be served in different ways, at different points in the meal. Consider slipping one of these dishes in as a first course or serving a duo as a main course. You'll find each eminently adaptable!

Clarified Butter

Clarified butter is unsalted butter that is melted and then cooled. Milk solids that sink to the bottom and proteins that float to the top are removed, leaving a pure, deep golden butterfat that has a high burn point and a sweet, nutty flavor. Use clarified butter in any dish where you want to cook ingredients in butter at a high heat.

Clarified butter will keep for about one month in an airtight container, refrigerated.

Curried Belgian Endive with Cashews

🌺 *Makes 4 servings*

Belgian endive is a winter staple on my table, where I serve it in a wide variety of ways. For such a modest vegetable it is incredibly versatile, offering up a host of different flavors and textures depending on how it is prepared.

Here Belgian endive is braised with Indian spices and raw cashews, and the alchemy in the pan makes this dish irresistible. The raw cashews absorb some of the cooking liquid and take on a meaty texture. The endive softens to a melting texture and then becomes lightly caramelized as the dish finishes cooking. Serve this as a first course or alongside steamed or grilled fish.

1 tablespoon extra virgin olive oil

2 teaspoons yellow mustard seeds

1 tablespoon curry powder, preferably from Madras

1 pound (500 g) medium Belgian endives, trimmed and cut in half lengthwise

1 garlic clove, thinly sliced lengthwise

½ cup (70 g) raw cashews

Fleur de sel

Note: *Endives hold heat, and are blistering hot when first removed from the heat. Let them sit and cool for at least 5 minutes before serving. Either yellow or black mustard seeds may be used. The black seeds taste nuttier than the yellow ones.*

1. Place the olive oil in a large, heavy skillet over medium heat. Add the mustard seeds and cook, stirring, until they begin to pop around in the pan. Add the curry powder and stir. Place the endives in the pan, cut side down, and cover them with water. Sprinkle the garlic over the endives, then the cashews, and stir. Finally, sprinkle the endives with the salt, cover, and cook for 10 minutes. Turn the endives and continue cooking them, covered, until they are tender but still resist a bit at the center, about 10 additional minutes.

2. Continue to let them cook, with the cover off, until the liquid has all evaporated and the endives begin to sizzle and turn golden, about 5 minutes. Remove them from the heat and let them cool for about 5 minutes before serving.

Roasted Eggplant and Hazelnut Caviar

🌿 *Makes about 1½ cups (75 g)*

This dish is rife with the flavor of hazelnuts, which plays off the tender texture of roasted eggplant. Combine this dish with several others from this chapter to make a meal or serve it in its rightful role as a side dish for roast fish or meat. As is typical for eggplant, this preparation is both elegant and casual, its toothsome meaty and tender texture like that of caponata.

Note: *When buying eggplants, choose those that are very firm and shiny, good indications of freshness. Many recipes call for eggplant to be sprinkled with salt and left to drain, a cure for the bitterness sometimes found in eggplant. If your eggplant is firm and shiny, thus fresh, it doesn't need salting.*

1. Preheat the oven to 450°F (230°C).

2. Roast the eggplants until they are tender when pierced with a fork, about 40 minutes. Remove from the oven and, as soon as they are cool enough to handle, peel them and coarsely chop the flesh.

3. While the eggplants are roasting, place the garlic, lemon zest, cilantro leaves, and salt in a mortar and mash the ingredients together with a pestle until they are quite homogenous. Drizzle in the hazelnut oil and lemon juice. Add the eggplant and ground hazelnuts and continue to mash with the pestle until the mixture is chunky but homogenous. Season to taste and serve.

- 2 firm, medium eggplants (about 11 ounces/310 g each), rinsed and pricked all over with a fork
- 1 garlic clove, coarsely chopped
- Zest of ½ lemon, minced
- ½ cup cilantro leaves
- Generous pinch of fine sea salt
- 1 tablespoon hazelnut oil, preferably Leblanc brand
- 1 tablespoon freshly squeezed lemon juice
- 1 tablespoon hazelnuts, lightly toasted and finely ground

Quinoa with Macadamia Nuts

Makes 6 servings

What makes quinoa extraordinary is its light, crunchy texture and its delicately nutty flavor. I cook it a lot because somehow it's more exciting, more interesting, just the tiniest bit less predictable, than any other grain I know. Add its uncommonly high protein content and you've got a near-perfect food.

Nuts go perfectly with quinoa, as do herbs and nut oils, as here. I hope you will make this often and adapt it to flavors and textures of your choosing. You can serve quinoa in place of rice, and you can have fun with it as well. My favorite way to serve it is to press it gently into a heart-shaped mold and turn it out onto a plate.

1 cup (195 g) quinoa

1 fresh bay leaf from the *Laurus nobilis* or dried imported bay leaf

¼ teaspoon fine sea salt

2 teaspoons lightly toasted sesame oil

⅓ cup (50 g) macadamia nuts, lightly toasted and diced

Fresh herbs such as tarragon, thyme, fennel fronds, or garlic chive tips for garnish (optional)

Note: *If the macadamia nuts are raw, toast them by preheating the oven to 400°F (200°C). Place the nuts in an ovenproof pan and toast them until you begin to smell a toasty aroma and they begin to turn golden brown, about 8 minutes. Remove from the heat and cool. If all you can find are roasted salted macadamias, use them as long as they are sweet and fresh tasting. Be careful not to add any salt to the quinoa until you've carefully stirred in the presalted macadamia nuts.*

The recipe calls for light sesame oil, which refers to the delicate flavor; Leblanc brand (see page 99) is ideal here.

Rinse the quinoa well to remove the bitter saponins that coat it.

1. Rinse the quinoa under cold running water until the water runs clear. Place the quinoa in a medium pan and add 2 cups (500 ml) water, the bay leaf, and the salt. Cover, bring the water to a boil over medium-high heat, reduce the heat so the water is simmering merrily, and cook until the quinoa is tender, about 12 minutes. Remove the quinoa from the heat and let it sit, covered, for at least 10 minutes and up to 20, to allow the quinoa to fluff up. Remove the bay leaf.

2. Just before serving, fold the sesame oil into the quinoa, using a large rubber scraper or large spoon. Fold in the macadamias and taste for seasoning.

3. To serve, using a ½-cup (125-ml) ramekin as a mold, mold the quinoa by simply packing it into the ramekin and then turning it out onto a very warm dinner plate. Garnish with the fresh herbs, if desired, and serve. Alternatively, serve using a large spoon.

Butternut Squash with Leeks and Pecans

Winter squash combined with leeks, lemon zest, and pecans makes this dish an ode to the season. I enjoyed but didn't swoon over butternut squash until local farmer Baptiste Bourdon began cultivating it several years ago. Now it's a favorite; I savor it as much for its fine texture and delicate flavor as for its familiarity. Because it is a relatively unknown squash in France, Baptiste has had to do some serious marketing to get his customers to buy it, and I love hearing him describe the virtues of "boot-air-noot."

Whichever squash you decide to use here, make sure it is fresh and local.

1 tablespoon (15 g) unsalted butter

1 tablespoon extra virgin olive oil

2 large leeks, thoroughly cleaned, trimmed, and cut into rounds ¼ inch (.6 cm) thick

Fine sea salt

1 small (2-pound/1-kg), firm winter squash, such as butternut, red kuri, ambercup, or hubbard, peeled, seeded, and cut into ½-inch (1.25-cm) cubes (to give 6 cups cubes)

Zest of 1 lemon, preferably organic, minced

⅓ cup (3 g) flat-leaf parsley leaves

Note: *Despite being hardy, most varieties of squash are delicate and cook more quickly than you think they will. Handle it gently, and stay close to the stove as it cooks so it doesn't overcook.*

1. Place the butter and the olive oil in a large skillet over medium heat. As the butter melts, stir it with the oil. As soon as the fats coat the bottom of the pan, add the leeks, stir to coat them with butter and oil, season lightly with salt, cover, and cook, stirring regularly, until the leeks are tender and slightly golden on the edges, about 8 minutes. Add the squash, lemon zest, and 3 tablespoons water and stir so the squash is thoroughly moistened. Season lightly with salt, cover, and cook, occasionally stirring very carefully to avoid breaking up the squash and adding water a tablespoon at a time if needed to

⅓ cup (40 g) pecans, lightly
toasted and coarsely chopped

keep the squash from sticking to the bottom of the pan, until the squash is tender through, 15 to 18 minutes.

2. Mince the parsley, remove the squash from the heat, and fold in the parsley and pecans. Season to taste and transfer to a serving bowl. Serve immediately.

Gorgeous Green Spinach with New Garlic

🌿 *Makes 4 servings*

Gorgeous is the only word to describe this spinach dish. It is simply perfectly fresh spinach wilted and dressed in the most ethereal, delicate dressing imaginable, yet it is so satisfying that you may want to make it the centerpiece of the meal.

New garlic is simply garlic that has been harvested before it is fully mature, when the cloves are still plump with juice, their skins not yet dried to the papery quality we expect from garlic. Its flavor is hot and fresh, its texture like a firm apple. If you can't find new garlic, good quality dried garlic is fine.

1 tablespoon soy sauce

2 teaspoons sake

½ teaspoon toasted sesame oil

½ teaspoon sugar

1 medium-sized new garlic clove, peeled

1 pound (500 g) spinach, stemmed and rinsed

2 tablespoons sesame seeds, lightly toasted

Note: *Sesame seeds can be found either hulled or unhulled. Hulled sesame seeds are ivory and slightly shiny and rather flat. Unhulled sesame seeds tend to be brown, although they can be red or black, depending on the variety. The unhulled seeds are very delicate to the tooth; the hulled seeds give a slight pop when you bite into them. They can be used interchangeably. When toasting hulled sesame seeds watch out, for the seeds will pop around, sometimes right out of the pan. I cover the pan with a splatter screen to keep them from escaping.*

1. Combine the soy sauce, sake, sesame oil, and sugar in a bowl; mix well. Mince the garlic and stir it into the sauce.

2. Steam the spinach in the water that clings to its leaves until the leaves are bright green and still retain some of their shape, about 3 minutes. Drain, then squeeze gently to extract some of the liquid. Transfer the spinach to a cutting board. Coarsely chop.

3. Whisk the soy sauce mixture and add the spinach. Toss until the spinach is thoroughly coated with the sauce.

4. To serve, either divide the spinach among four small bowls or serve as a side dish. Sprinkle with the toasted sesame seeds and serve.

Potatoes with Yogurt and Pistachios

🍀 *Makes 6 servings*

This dish is a part of the treasure trove of the cuisine of Anatonia, from the long, narrow Fertile Crescent of Turkey. Rich with pistachio nuts, the region's pride, and lively with the local herbs and spices, this dish—and the cuisine it comes from—is a mix of the hearty and the ethereal.

Although included in the side-dish chapter, this dish easily makes a meal, with a crisp green salad alongside. It is also an ideal accompaniment to the Pistachio- and Pepper-Stuffed Lamb Fillet (page 126).

2 pounds (1 kg) whole-milk
    yogurt

1 large egg

1 tablespoon unbleached
    all-purpose flour

1 large garlic clove, minced

Fine sea salt and freshly ground
    black pepper

2 pounds (1 kg) small waxy or
    new potatoes, scrubbed

1 tablespoon clarified butter
    (page 108)

1 tablespoon extra virgin olive oil

½ teaspoon saffron threads,
    crushed

1 medium onion, thinly sliced

⅓ cup (55 g) pistachios

Mint Oil (page 238) for garnish

Note: *Don't try to substitute low-fat or nonfat yogurt; neither will work.*

The point of the clarified butter here is its nutty flavor and high burn point. If you don't have clarified butter, use regular butter and watch it carefully, as it will brown more quickly than clarified butter.

1. Place the yogurt in a cheesecloth-lined sieve set over a bowl and let it drain for about 4 hours. The yogurt will be quite thick, about the consistency of soft cream cheese. Transfer the yogurt to a medium saucepan. Whisk in the egg, flour, and garlic and bring to a boil over medium-high heat. Reduce the heat so the yogurt mixture is boiling gently and cook until the mixture thickens and the flavor of the flour is gone, 2 to 3 minutes. Remove from the heat, season with salt and pepper, and reserve.

2. Place a steamer over medium-high heat and, when the water is boiling, place the potatoes in the steamer, cover, and steam the potatoes until they are tender through, about 18 minutes. Remove from the heat and reserve.

When the potatoes are cool enough to handle, peel them. If they aren't small, cut them into 1½-inch (4-cm) chunks.

3. Melt the clarified butter with the olive oil in a large skillet over medium-high heat. When the butter begins to melt, add the saffron and stir. Cook the saffron until it begins to sizzle and smell like heaven, then add the onion and stir. Cook until the onions soften at the edges, about 8 minutes, then add the potatoes and stir them into the onion. Season with salt and continue cooking, stirring and shaking the pan often, until the onion is thoroughly softened and the potatoes begin to brown around the edges, about 10 minutes. Add the yogurt sauce to the potatoes, stir, then add the pistachios and stir them into the sauce. Cook, stirring and shaking the pan, until all the ingredients are combined thoroughly and heated through, about 8 minutes. Remove from the heat.

4. To serve, either evenly divide the potatoes among six warmed plates and drizzle with equal amounts of mint oil or pass the potatoes and the mint oil separately.

Parsnip and Walnut Fricassee

🍀 *Makes 2 main-course servings or 4 side-dish servings*

Parsnips are a sweet, old-fashioned vegetable, one my grandmother and my father both adored. Instead of the humble staple it was in those generations, though, the parsnip has become a specialty vegetable, something vaunted and chic to cook and eat. If chic is what it takes to get this vegetable back on the table, then I'm all for it. One thing I know for certain is that even the most skeptical of eaters succumbs to the haunting, sweet, buttery flavor and texture of parsnips.

I do my very best to support the parsnip, and the parsnip growers of the world, serving it at every opportunity. This is a favorite preparation, which can either leave the parsnip in its habitual supporting role or make it the main character. Serve this alongside a grilled steak or lamb chops or put it center stage as a first course.

1 pound (500 g) parsnips, trimmed and peeled

1 tablespoon walnut oil

1 garlic clove, minced

2 tablespoons walnuts, coarsely chopped

½ teaspoon fresh thyme leaves, or to taste

Fine sea salt and freshly ground black pepper

Note: *When buying parsnips, which look like stubby white carrots, look for those that are unblemished and evenly ivory in color. They must be firm and look as though they were harvested recently.*

Walnut oil is fragile, so the heat in this recipe is delicate, to preserve the oil's finest qualities.

1. Cut the parsnips lengthwise into quarters and cut out the tough core. Cut the parsnip quarters into 1-inch lengths.

2. Bring a medium pan of salted water to a boil and add the parsnips. Return the water to a boil and cook the parsnips until tender through, about 8 minutes. Drain the parsnips.

3. In a heavy nonstick skillet over medium-low heat, warm the walnut oil and garlic until the garlic is sizzling.

Add the parsnips, walnuts, and fresh thyme leaves and cook, stirring frequently and shaking the pan, until the parsnips are light gold and all the ingredients are hot through, about 8 minutes. Season the parsnips with salt and pepper, toss and stir to combine, then serve.

Nutty Fresh Shell Beans

✿ Makes 6 servings

Fresh shell beans are grown for the seed rather than for the pod. Their season is fleeting—just a couple of short months. Harbingers of autumn, they usually appear at the farmers' market at the very tip-end of summer, when temperatures begin to be chilly in the morning but days are still full and warm. The first to arrive in my market are speckled red *haricots à ecossais*, called *tongue of fire beans* in the United States. Then come the pale yellow podded version, which we just call *shell beans*, then the gorgeously pale white Paimpol beans.

Whenever they are cooked and eaten, their natural affinity for nuts and nut oils never wanes. As for herbs, savory or rosemary complements them best. I hope you'll add these to your repertoire.

3 pounds (1.5 kg) shell beans in the pod, shucked

Several sprigs of fresh rosemary or savory

2 tablespoons hazelnut oil

Sea salt and freshly ground black pepper

Fleur de sel

Fresh rosemary sprigs for garnish

Note: *Shell and place the beans in sturdy plastic bags, then put them in the freezer. They will keep for many months and can be cooked from their frozen state. Once frozen, they are best added to soups or stews rather than prepared as a separate side dish.*

Try these with hazelnut oil, as suggested here, then sample them with other nut oils as well.

Another serving suggestion is to toss these in walnut oil and then top each serving with a freshly sautéed piece of foie gras.

1. Bring a large pot of salted water to a boil. Add the beans and 2 to 3 sprigs of herbs and cook, covered, until the beans are just tender through, about 15 minutes. Keep warm in the water until ready to serve.

2. Just before serving, discard the herbs, drain the beans, and transfer the warm beans to a medium bowl. Toss with the hazelnut oil and season with salt and pepper. Remove the leaves from the remaining herbs, coarsely chop them, and add to the beans. Toss well and place an equal amount in each of six warmed shallow bowls. Season with the fleur de sel and garnish with the rosemary sprigs at the last minute.

Sautéed Carrots East Indian Style

🍀 *Makes 4 servings*

India is the world's largest producer of cashews. On the trees, cashews look like a big comma hanging from the bottom of a bulbous fruit called a *cashew apple.* Considering the work involved in getting the cashew from its dual shells (and avoiding a very caustic oil that resides between them), their price should rival that of the gold standard. They are very available and affordable, however, and here they combine with spices to make carrots seem like something exotic and more than just delicious. I serve this with roast chicken that I've rubbed under the skin with some curry powder.

2 tablespoons extra virgin olive oil

1 teaspoon black mustard seeds

4 large carrots (about 6 ounces/180 g each), trimmed, peeled, and cut into ¼-inch (.6-cm) cubes

2 shallots, minced

½ teaspoon ground cumin

Generous ¼ teaspoon ground turmeric

1 bird's-eye or other hot chile

3 tablespoons unsweetened shredded coconut

Fine sea salt

¼ cup (40 g) cashews, lightly toasted and coarsely chopped

Note: *Be sure to remove the hot chile before you serve this dish. These carrots are also good at room temperature.*

1. Heat the olive oil in a medium saucepan over medium heat and sauté the mustard seeds. They'll jump and pop all over the place, so cover the pan with a splatter screen and shake it to move them around. Add the carrots, shallots, spices, chile, and coconut, stir, and add about ¼ teaspoon salt. Add ½ cup (125 ml) water, bring it to a simmer, and cook the carrots, covered, until they are tender, checking after about 10 minutes to be sure the water hasn't evaporated. If it has, and the carrots aren't quite tender through, add another ½ cup (125 ml) water and continue cooking. The carrots should cook for approximately 20 minutes total.

2. Remove the cover and stir in the cashews. Continue cooking the carrots, uncovered, stirring occasionally, until all the water has evaporated, about 4 minutes. Remove from the heat, remove and discard the chile, season to taste, and serve.

Brussels Sprouts and Potatoes with Poppy Seed Dressing

❧ *Makes 4 to 6 servings*

My children and I are ravenous Brussels sprout eaters. I steam and braise them, roast and sauté them, even occasionally separate their little leaves and dress them in a vinaigrette to eat raw.

Combined with potatoes as they are here, their sweet flavor emerges more than ever. When dressed with the poppy seed dressing, the combination turns into something very special.

Note: *Brussels sprouts must be very, very fresh or their flavor will be bitter. Marion Pruitt, who tests my recipes, used frozen Brussels sprouts when making this. Her comment: "What a surprise! These frozen gems were much better than anything I've had this year . . . tender, sweet, with a clean, fresh taste!" It makes sense, since the vegetables are flash frozen shortly after harvest.*

- 1 pound (450 g) potatoes that are both waxy and starchy, such as Yukon Gold, peeled and cut into 1-inch (2.5-cm) cubes
- 2 teaspoons coarse sea salt
- 1 pound (450 g) Brussels sprouts, trimmed and cut in half lengthwise
- 3 tablespoons Poppy Seed Dressing (page 232)
- Fine sea salt and freshly ground black pepper

1. Place the potatoes in a saucepan and just cover with water. Add the coarse salt, bring the water to a boil, reduce to a simmer, and cook the potatoes until they are tender through, 12 to 15 minutes. Remove from the heat and keep warm.

2. Bring 3 cups (750 ml) water to a boil in the bottom half of a steamer. Place the Brussels sprouts over the steaming water and steam just until they are tender all the way through but still have their bright green color, about 8 minutes.

3. Place the Brussels sprouts and the potatoes in a large bowl. Drizzle with the poppy seed dressing, then carefully fold the dressing into the vegetables until they are coated thoroughly. Season with salt and pepper and serve immediately.

Spiced Rice with Toasty Nuts

🌸 *Makes 6 servings*

This delicate dish, inspired by a blend of spices commonly used in India, fills the kitchen with its exotic aromas. I serve it as a side dish with grilled fish or as part of a vegetarian meal, along with the Butternut Squash and Arugula Salad (page 96).

Note: *Don't skip soaking and draining the rice; these steps make the rice more tender and light.*

To crack the cardamom, roll over them with a rolling pin several times, until their fragrance is released. Then add them whole to the rice.

You can serve the rice with the garnishes passed alongside, though I prefer serving it with the garnish on top for its lovely presentation.

Unsweetened coconut is available at health food and specialty stores.

1. Rinse the rice under cold running water until the water runs clear. Soak the rice in cool water for 30 minutes and then drain it for 30 minutes.

2. Melt the clarified butter in a heatproof medium casserole over medium heat. Add all the whole spices and cook until the air is filled with their aroma and they begin to turn golden, 1 to 2 minutes. Add the turmeric and stir, then add the rice and cook, stirring, until it is nearly translucent, about 3 minutes. Slowly stir in 5 cups (1.25 l) very hot water and the salt. Cover and cook the rice until it is tender, about 20 minutes.

3. While the rice is cooking, prepare the garnish. Melt 2 tablespoons clarified butter in a heavy skillet over

2½ cups (400 g) basmati rice

2 tablespoons clarified butter (page 108)

6 cardamom pods, cracked

One 4-inch (10-cm) cinnamon stick

1 star anise

2 cloves

20 whole black peppercorns

½ teaspoon ground turmeric

1 teaspoon fine sea salt

FOR THE GARNISH:

2 to 3 tablespoons clarified butter (page 108)

3 medium onions, sliced paper-thin

2 teaspoons black mustard seeds

⅔ cup cashews or peanuts

Fine sea salt

½ cup (4 g) cilantro leaves, lightly packed

medium heat. Add the onions and mustard seeds and cook, stirring, until the onions are deep golden and crisp and the mustard seeds pop, about 10 minutes. Remove from the pan. Add the remaining tablespoon of butter to the pan if necessary, then add the nuts, sprinkle with salt and cook, stirring, until they are golden, about 7 minutes. Transfer the nuts to a small bowl. Mince the cilantro and add it to the nuts, tossing to mix well. Reserve.

⅓ cup (28 g) unsweetened shredded coconut

4. Remove the lid from the rice pan and let it sit for 2 to 3 minutes. Remove the whole spices, fluff up the rice with a fork, and either transfer it to a warmed serving dish or leave it in the pan. Top it with the garnishes, one after the other, or serve them separately, immediately, while the rice is very hot and the garnishes are very fresh.

Gaziantep and Food

Gaziantep, Turkey, sits on the western border of the Fertile Crescent of eastern Anatolia, a flat region of rich fields and arid plains ringed by foothills. Crossed by the Tigris and the Euphrates, punctuated by the drama of Ataturk's dam and Mount Nemrut with its haunting temple ruins and huge stone heads, it is that conundrum of an ancient region in development. Its people practice agrarian and artisan principles honed over centuries; its cities and towns burst with energy, and a common dream is to join the West, in the form of the European Economic Community.

Western-style development in Gaziantep shows in the neighborhoods of stocky, multi-storied apartment buildings surrounded by traffic-choked streets. A lack of aesthetics is made up for by environmental consciousness; each building has a forest of solar panels on its roof, and residents rarely resort to any other type of power.

Tucked into the center of all this is the ancient quarter of lovely white homes and shops, sinuous and climbing cobbled streets, cafés, and pastry shops. The heart of it is El-maci Pazari, a cacophonous market of narrow, covered alleys and streetside shops whose wares spill out onto the uneven sidewalks. Between vendors and hagglers, the constant, steady tapping of tin and silversmiths, the cars and scooters, noise issues from everywhere, punctuated by the occasional shout of a particularly vociferous vendor. Money and goods change hands with blurry speed; boys balancing trays piled with delicate etched glasses and pots of mint tea run through the crowds, stopping at a whistle or a call to pour some in exchange for a few pennies before racing off again. Mint tea is offered by merchants to conclude a deal large or small. Thus, everywhere amid the bustle are tranquil, tea-sipping moments.

Markets are rich with the aromas of spices and the overwhelming scent of peppers, which are a signature of Gaziantep cuisine. Strings of them, bright red and sun-dried, hang from shop ceilings and walls; baskets hold the same peppers ground to a rough powder, and wide bowls offer thick, sticky *biber salcasi*, a sweet-to-searing paste made from the peppers.

Second only to peppers in quantity and variety are nuts, displayed in huge jute bags or smaller wildly colored ones that sit right on the floor. The pistachio is queen, for Gaziantep is the center of Turkey's pistachio-producing region. Her suitors are the walnut, the almond, the pine nut, the hazelnut, and an array of toasted seeds. Women, many dressed in the body-shielding manto and head-covering esarp, and men, often wearing the baggy shalwar pants, nibble constantly on nuts and seeds as they go about their business.

Just outside Gaziantep, spare, dry fields and rolling hills stretch on forever, the soil chunky red and iron-rich. Gnarled pistachio trees are planted alongside olive trees and grapevines so there is always a crop to harvest, no matter the year or atmospheric conditions.

I'm in a tiny car with Kamil Sarpkaya, a research scientist with Gaziantep's pistachio research station. A solid young man with a mass of deep brown corkscrew hair, he perspires with pistachio passion, particularly the growing and treating of the trees. How to explain this passion? He says he cannot; he's got it, it consumes his life, it has him taking an afternoon off to share it with me. Fortunately we have a driver, Naci Gulgun, so Kamil's hands are free to make line drawings in my notebook to illustrate the life cycle of the pistachio tree, the way the trees are planted, the way they are trimmed, the way the nuts develop and grow, and any other fact that comes to his mind.

We see a crew in one of the pistachio orchards lining the road, and Kamil signals Mr. Gulgun to stop. We get out and, defying overloaded trucks careening down the road on their way to the city, run to the other side and hastily clamber over the guardrail.

"The germ plasm of the pistachio is here, right here," Kamil said, gently stamping his feet in the red soil. "This is where it began."

Kamil strikes up a conversation with Hussein Turan, the field owner, and his crew. I stand in the shadow of these men whose skin is burnished the color of red oak, their hair abundantly black and thick, their eyes and smiles open and frank. They are curious about what might have caused us to stop and run to their field, yet at ease with our presence.

The trees surrounding us remind me of suffering sculptures, their gnarled limbs reaching out as though starving—for air, for water, for sustenance. Their bark is like skin. Thin and silvery. I know if I touch it, it will be warm. Mr. Turan leads me right up to one and, indeed, when my fingers slide along the bark it is warm, as though sap were coursing just below the surface. It turns out that the pistachio trees look as if they suffer because they do. It takes ten to fifteen years for a tree to produce enough nuts to harvest, in part because the roots must pierce a layer of porous rock below the surface of the red soil. Once the smaller female trees are in produc-

tion, they produce in a three-year cycle with one productive year, one nonproductive year, and one year that yields a small production. A wild pistachio will have random production cycles; those planted together like the ones in this field self-regulate so their productive years coincide.

According to Kamil, yields could increase substantially, and "off" years could become productive if growers would irrigate. "They use their beliefs to grow pistachio nuts," he said. "And belief has it that irrigation will kill the pistachio tree." He shakes his head with frustration. "I tell them it isn't true, but they don't trust me yet. I'm from Ankara, and I've been here for only two years; it will take time."

I learn from these men that the nuts they've just finished harvesting by hand, one bunch at a time, are destined for the snack market. One of the workers gives me a handful, and I open one—it is fat, pale yellow, and slightly crisp with an exquisite, browned butter flavor.

It is October, and the harvest has been going on since June. At that early date, the pistachios are embryonic, with all of their adult savor and color concentrated in a kernel that is a fraction of its adult size. Called "green gold," these small, electric green kernels that are covered with a fine, grayish white film are prized for Gaziantep's famed pastries, which include buttery-crisp baklava, *katmer*—also called the "whirling dervish pancake" because of the way the dough is thrown and twirled into the air to get its paper-thin texture and pizza-round shape—and jellied *loukoum*. Each tree yields about 100 pounds of the immature nut and about 50 pounds of the larger, more mature nut.

The pistachio has three hulls to protect the meat inside. The first is very hard, and according to Kamil, the growers spread them out and drive a truck over them to crack it off. Underneath is a wrinkled rosy sheath, which either drops off or is removed by machine in small factories set up in and around Gaziantep. Under that is the ivory shell we know, most of which pop open in the fields, within their protective coverings. Any nuts that haven't opened naturally are sent out into the countryside, where women crack them open by hand, using tiny, etched nutcrackers destined for that purpose.

The workers' day is finished. They politely say good-bye with smiles and nodding heads, then take themselves to a large old wagon piled with nut-filled crates and climb in, sitting wherever they can balance. The owner steps up into the aging tractor to pull them home. We all wave good-bye as the tractor lurches out of sight amid the trees.

Kamil, Mr. Gulgun, and I clamber back over the guardrail, run across the death-defying highway, and settle back into our sleek little car as two worlds separate.

Desserts

Lemon Poppy Seed Ice Cream

Kabili Fruit and Nut Squares

Almond Blancmange

Coconut Sticky Rice with Peanuts

Hazelnut Sablés—Sand Cookies

Wenatchee Apple Torte

Joanne's Pfefferneuse—Spiced
Walnut and Almond Cookies

Lemon Madeleines with Pistachios

Lena's Nut Cookies

Hazelnut Cakes—Financiers

Coconut, Pistachio, and Chocolate
Macaroons

Rocky Road

Peanut and Sesame Brittle

Pistachio Ice Cream

Nougat Glacé

Jacqueline's Walnut Cake

Golden Pound Cake Crowned with
Nuts

Lena's Poppy Seed Cake

Fiona's Yogurt Cake

Crumbly Almond Cake—Sbrisolona

Walnut Coffee Tourte with
Coffee Frosting

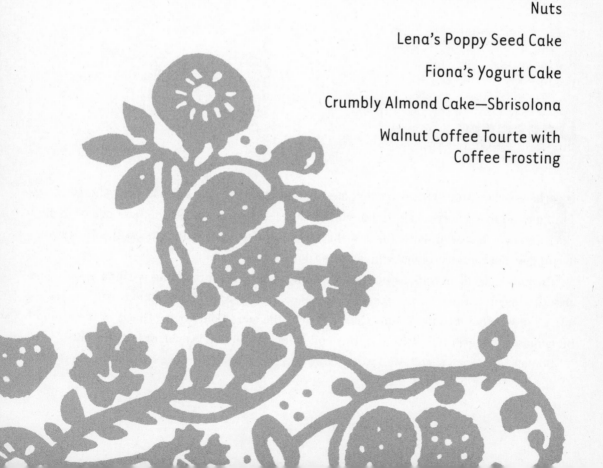

Desserts

There are no gray areas when it comes to dessert—everyone loves it. Well, almost everyone. I have a very close friend who eschews sweets of every kind, and occasionally I find myself searching for the flaw that has caused this particular peccadillo. He's a wonderful guy; but for his problem with sweets I'd think him perfect.

Prevailing wisdom tells us perfection is impossible. But prevailing wisdom is only just about to become aware of the desserts in this collection, and I am certain it will change its mind. For whether it be the Walnut Coffee Tourte, the incredible Nougat Glacé, or the Almond Blancmange, or any other dessert in this collection, perfection is evident in every bite.

So delve in, forget that flawed world out there, and revel in these perfect nut desserts!

Lemon Poppy Seed Ice Cream

🌿 *Makes 1 quart (1 liter)*

What's even better than the dusky rich poppy seed flavor and the tang of lemon here is the crisp "pop!" the seeds make when you bite into them—it makes every mouthful a noisy little adventure. Because this isn't a cooked custard ice cream, it takes minutes to put together, so keep the ingredients on hand. If the half-and-half and the lemons are chilled (store your lemons in the refrigerator; they'll keep longer), this can be a very impromptu dessert, as the mixture will need virtually no time to chill.

Note: *Pulverizing the lemon zest with the sugar brings out the oils in the zest, to intensify the lemony flavor of the ice cream.*

- Zest of 2 lemons
- 1½ cups (300 g) sugar
- ⅓ cup (80 ml) freshly squeezed lemon juice
- 1 quart (1 liter) half-and-half
- ¼ cup (35 g) poppy seeds

1. Place the lemon zest and sugar in a food processor. Process until the sugar and zest are thoroughly combined, and the sugar is a bit damp from the oil in the zest. Add the lemon juice and process to blend.

2. Scrape the sugar and lemon mixture into a large non-reactive bowl. Whisk in the half-and-half until combined, then whisk in the poppy seeds. To allow the flavors to meld, refrigerate for at least 1 hour and up to 1 day.

3. Before freezing, whisk the mixture so it is combined thoroughly, then freeze it in an ice cream maker following the manufacturer's instructions.

Kabili Fruit and Nut Squares

🍀 Makes 12 servings

This recipe comes from a woman I met whose first name is Malika, a lovely blue-eyed blond from the Kabil region of Algeria. Fragrant with fruit and nuts, and the ubiquitous orange flower water of North African pastries, it is always a welcome dessert. I made it one night for a dinner that I had catered by an Algerian friend, Cherifa Kalabi, and she begged for the recipe. Cherifa is from Algiers and had never tasted this Kabili confection!

1 recipe Sweet Pie Pastry (page 235)

3 tablespoons (45 g) unsalted butter

¼ cup plus 2 tablespoons (90 ml) unfiltered honey

⅔ cup (100 g) raw almonds, skinned, lightly toasted, and coarsely chopped

⅔ cup (100 g) hazelnuts, lightly toasted, skinned, and coarsely chopped

½ cup dates (100 g), pitted and thinly sliced lengthwise

Scant ½ teaspoon fleur de sel

2 tablespoons orange flower water

Note: *These squares truly are better when made several hours in advance and left to ripen. They will also keep for several days in an airtight container. If you cannot find orange flower water locally, I highly recommend you order some from the Spice House, thespicehouse.com.*

1. Preheat the oven to 400°F (200°C).

2. Roll out the pastry to a thickness of about ¼ inch (.6 cm) to make a rectangle about 7 × 13 inches (18 × 33 cm). Transfer the pastry to a jelly-roll pan by rolling it tightly around the rolling pin, then unrolling it onto the pan. Bake it in the center of the oven until the pastry is golden at the edges and nearly baked through, about 13 minutes. Remove from the oven and reserve.

3. Reduce the oven temperature to 375°F (190°C).

4. In a large, heavy saucepan, over medium heat, heat the butter with the honey. Add the chopped nuts and the dates and cook, stirring, just until the nuts are coated with the honey. Remove from the heat, add the fleur de sel and orange flower water, and stir until mixed. Then spread the nuts atop the prebaked pastry, going as close to the edge as you can. Drizzle the nuts with any honey and butter left in the pan.

5. Place the pan in the center of the oven and bake until the edges of the pastry and the nuts are deep golden, about 8 minutes. Remove from the oven and let cool, then cut the pastry into 12 serving pieces.

Almond Blancmange

🍀 *Makes 6 servings*

This very old-fashioned dessert is made by soaking almonds, then grinding them, then squeezing all the precious milk you can from them. Combine the almond milk with sugar, a touch of almond extract, and some gelatin and you've got a unique dessert. I serve this in a stemmed glass with a bit of homemade black or red currant jelly in the bottom for a spot of color and a little hit of tart-sweet right at the end. Try this with fresh, seasonal fruit such as thinly sliced strawberries or raspberries alongside. Good, too, are ripe persimmons, cherries, or peaches.

2 teaspoons powdered gelatin or 4 gelatin leaves

Scant 3 cups (about 700 ml) fresh Almond Milk (page 233)

¾ cup (150 g) sugar

½ teaspoon almond extract

2 tablespoons red or black currant jelly

Fresh mint or basil leaves for garnish (optional)

Note: *Often the dessert version of blancmange has cream whipped into the almond gelatin. This version does not, and the flavor attests to its purity, which is what I love about it. If you feel the lack of cream, go ahead and use some as a garnish.*

This recipe calls for homemade almond milk, but you can also buy it at food co-ops or health food stores.

1. If using gelatin leaves, place them in a small bowl and cover with cold water.

2. Place the almond milk and sugar in a medium saucepan over very low heat and stir until the milk is just hot. Do not boil the almond milk. Continue stirring until the sugar is dissolved, then remove from the heat. If using powdered gelatin, slowly sprinkle the powder into the sweetened almond milk as you whisk. If using gelatin leaves, squeeze the water from a leaf and whisk it slowly into the almond milk. Repeat with all the leaves of gelatin. Remove the mixture from the heat, stir in the almond extract, and let the mixture cool to room temperature.

3. Evenly divide the jelly among six wineglasses. Pour the almond mixture atop the jelly and refrigerate until the mixture gels, 4 to 6 hours. You can also prepare this dessert the night before you plan to serve it.

4. To serve, either top the blancmange with fruit, if using small berries, or serve the fruit alongside. If serving the fruit alongside, garnish each dessert with a mint or basil leaf.

Coconut Sticky Rice with Peanuts

🍀 *Makes 6 to 8 servings*

In Thailand sticky rice is the equivalent of bread at Western meals. It's always on the table, from soup to dessert. This is a classic sticky rice dessert, with its topping of sweet and salty roasted peanuts, and such a treat that I find each time I serve it, eyes light up as spoons dip into it for that first sensuous, coconut-rich bite.

There are a few rules for making the Thai version of coconut sticky rice. It must always be pure white, so white sugar rather than palm sugar is used as a sweetener. Pandanus leaf, a vanilla-scented herb that is ubiquitous in Thai cooking, is the preferred flavoring; it can be found at Asian grocery stores.

The recipe calls for a garnish of bananas poached lightly in the coconut milk mixture, which is one of many possibilities. During mango season, try serving a mound of freshly sliced fruit, dripping with sweet juices, alongside the sticky rice, with a river of coconut milk poured over all. Sweet and salty roasted peanuts are one garnish; another is fried shallots (yes, for dessert); and another is coconut custard—your imagination is the only real limit.

2 cups (400 g) sticky rice

4½ cups (1.1 l) coconut milk

½ cup (100 g) granulated sugar, or to taste

½ teaspoon fine sea salt

1 pandanus leaf, cut into 2-inch (5-cm) lengths, or a 1-inch (2.5-cm) piece vanilla bean

FOR THE PEANUTS:

½ cup (80 g) peanuts, lightly toasted

Note: *The best coconut milk is fresh from a coconut. An excellent substitute, however, is UHT coconut milk, which comes in a rectangular carton. Barring that, try canned organic coconut milk. Coconut sticky rice is luscious for breakfast.*

1. Place the sticky rice in a sieve and wash it under cool running water until the water runs nearly clear. Place the rice in a bowl, cover it with water, and let soak overnight or for at least 8 hours.

2. Bring 3 cups (750 ml) water to a boil in the bottom half of a steamer. Place the rice in a conical colander lined with cheesecloth and place over the steaming water.

1 tablespoon palm sugar

½ teaspoon fleur de sel

FOR THE BANANAS:

2 bananas, cut into ¼-inch thick
(.6 cm) diagonal slices

Cover and steam until the rice is tender but not so soft it sticks together, 20 to 25 minutes. (If you don't have a conical bamboo steamer—readily available at most Asian groceries—use a flat-bottomed steamer or improvise with a colander.)

3. While the rice is cooking, place the coconut milk, granulated sugar, salt, and pandanus leaf or vanilla bean in a medium saucepan over medium heat. Heat just to simmer, stirring, until the sugar is dissolved. Be very careful not to boil the coconut cream. Remove from the heat and keep warm. Also remove the pandanus leaf or vanilla bean.

4. When the rice is steamed, place it in a bowl the right size for it to fill the bowl three-quarters full. Carefully spoon enough coconut cream mixture over it to cover the rice by 1 inch (2.5 cm). Cover and let sit until the rice has absorbed all of the coconut cream, about 25 minutes. Reserve the remaining coconut cream mixture.

5. While the rice is absorbing the coconut cream, prepare the peanuts. Place the peanuts and the palm sugar in a mortar and crush them together, using the pestle, until the peanuts are quite finely ground and thoroughly combined with the sugar. (You may do this in a food processor, making sure not to process the nuts and sugar into peanut butter.) Stir in the fleur de sel and transfer the mixture to a serving bowl.

6. Return the remaining coconut cream to the pan over low heat. Add the sliced bananas and heat the bananas until they are hot through, about 8 minutes. Do not boil the coconut cream.

7. To serve, fold the coconut sticky rice three or four times to thoroughly mix the coconut cream into it. Using a large spoon, spoon out the rice into shallow soup bowls. Top with equal amounts of the coconut banana mixture, then sprinkle with a generous amount of the peanuts and serve any remaining peanuts alongside as a garnish.

Ode to the Thai Countryside

As I rode around the village of Baan Mai, near the boisterous city of Chiang Mai, Thailand, with my friend Sunny Bovornat, a tour guide when he isn't an information scientist at Chiang Mai University, I felt as if I were in an eighteenth-century painting. Of course, I had to mentally airbrush out the motorbikes attached to small tractors and the vivid gold temple built at the edge of the village on land where an ancient temple had once stood. I also had to ignore that I was in a car, but all of that was easy with the backdrop of rice paddies, blue-coated, bamboo-hatted workers, their backs bent over to pull weeds, water buffalo meandering about, and the mist-wreathed hills in the distance.

Sunny was showing me his village and its environs to help me understand Thai cuisine. His mother cooked for the king of Thailand a generation ago, and he was conscripted into the kitchen early as he helped her chop and whisk. That early start fired him with passion, and he has become an expert in northern Thai cuisine. He cooks it, teaches it, and writes about it when he isn't eating it.

I had come to Thailand specifically to see the role that nuts played in its cuisine. Like most who enjoy Thai food, I was aware of the occasional cashew, but it wasn't until I'd eaten at a rousing restaurant in, of all places, Portland, Oregon, that I realized there was more to nuts in Thai food.

At Pok Pok, owner Andrew Ricker, who was probably Thai in another life but couldn't look more northern European with his bristle of red hair and generous sprinkling of freckles, has dedicated himself to re-creating Thai street food. Ricker, who spent years backpacking throughout Asia before settling on Chiang Mai as one of his favorite spots, asserts that Thai street food is the gastronomic pinnacle of the country's cuisine. After spending a week in and around Chiang Mai with him and Sunny eating everything we came across from dawn to well beyond dusk, I have to agree. And the nuts—oh, the nuts! If it wasn't peanuts—and it usually was—then it was cashews, or an odd and buttery little specimen called *bua kela*, which were roasted in tiny little ovens on the street.

The Thai peanut, which is either a Valencia or a Virginia variety, is not an important commercial crop in Thailand, yet most rural families have a plot they grow for their own consumption. History shows peanut production in Thailand as long ago as 400 years, though commercial production began in earnest 150 years ago. While you won't find peanut butter on a Thai menu or in a Thai grocery, you will find that the humble legume—for it isn't a nut at all—is boiled in the shell and eaten as a snack, ground and mixed with salt and sugar and then sprinkled on desserts, tucked into pork dumplings, sautéed with poultry and vegetables, folded into custards and sticky rice, fried and seasoned with fresh herbs, pounded to a paste and blended with peppers and herbs to make a savory, piquant sauce. Peanuts are important enough in Thai cuisine that the 135,000 tons produced there annually don't meet the demand. The country has

to import almost double that amount each year.

While in Chiang Mai I lost count of how many times we would pass a cart on a side street or a main thoroughfare offering some delicacy, and Sunny would jam on the brakes and fly out of the car, leaving it running, to return with a handful of plastic bags, each containing something delicious. What emerged from those bags, each disarmingly twisted closed so that not even one drop of liquid escaped, were delicacies the like of which I'd never tasted—roasted coconut milk, blends of herbs and rice, drippy coconut confections, salty-sweet meat mixtures, chunks of roasted coconut, miniature fish stews. When I exclaimed over a dish—which I believe I always did—Sunny promised to teach it to me.

He had the perfect kitchen in mind for the job. We decided to take a break from cacophonous Chiang Mai and after a meandering trip out of the city and into the countryside, which included a stop for a hot and garlicky bowl of beef noodles at a house-cum-café Sunny knew about, we arrived at a guest house and carried groceries into its rudimentary, open-air kitchen.

It was a simple room with nothing more than a bit of counter space, a jumble of bowls and pans, two large wok burners, a sink, and a few cleavers and utensils. I, who work in the most up-to-date professional home kitchen, was enchanted.

Sunny's first move was to pull out a large stone mortar and set it on the corner of a none-too-sturdy countertop. ("You always set a mortar and pestle over the leg of a counter," Andy pointed out. "That way the leg supports the pounding and the counter won't fall down.") He poured roasted peanuts into the mortar and showed me how to hold the pestle just so, firmly at one end so I could use its weight and my own force to pound ingredients to a paste. He waved me to get going, and I did, pounding over and over in what I learned is a time-honored gesture in Thailand and the beginning of just about every northern Thai dish.

As I pounded, the three of us talked when we could over the "pok pok" of the mortar and pestle, the spitting and frying in the wok, the sounds of monkeys screeching in the nearby forest. It was a warm day, but cool air wafted in the windows as the scent of browning garlic combined with the sweetness of coconut milk.

We needed to skin peanuts for one of our dishes, and Andy took me outside to show me the best method. He poured a handful high into the air over a bowl he held in one hand, blowing on the peanuts as they fell to make the skins fly away. I must have looked incredulous at this primitive method, for Andy stopped and looked at me with a quizzical "What? You think this is stupid? Let me tell you, there's no better way."

Laughing but plenty humbled, I joined him, dropping and blowing as Sunny stayed inside, preparing his special curry paste. We returned to the kitchen to fry, fold, and stir our way to an array of dishes that not only dazzled with their colors and aromas but demonstrated the importance of nuts to Thai cuisine. Together we made peanut sauce, bamboo-steamed sticky rice and whole fish, cashew chicken, lemony-tart green papaya salad, and fried shallot-rich pomelo salad.

Some hours later, my arm well exercised, my palate well singed with the intensity of flavors from the dishes we'd created, the three of us sat, sated, at an open-air table, the only light against the pitch black of the jungle outside a candle amid our now-empty plates and the dying light from the fire Sunny had built to steam the fish in a huge bamboo stalk.

Sunny had carefully crafted our menu so that I would learn an array of techniques and taste a wide palette of flavors. Andy had been both cooking partner and teacher, giving me a wealth of tricks and tips he's learned over the years in his quest to perfect the street food of his beloved Chiang Mai. I'd cooked and written furiously, tasted carefully, enjoyed immensely. Now, with the night mists falling amidst the squeaks and squawks of jungle creatures, our food-oriented conversation was falling to hushed comments as we sipped a Quercy I'd brought from France. It was a surprisingly perfect accompaniment to a cuisine that is often accompanied by locally produced rice rum, Coca-Cola, or beer.

In not too many hours the morning mists would rise and we would return to the kitchen. On the breakfast menu? A sweet coconut and peanut sticky rice dish. I couldn't imagine anything better with which to greet the day.

Hazelnut Sablés—Sand Cookies

🍀 *Makes about 110 1½-inch (4-cm) cookies*

These delicate cookies come to me from Edith Leroy, my acknowledged French sister and best early-morning swimming friend. Edith rarely lights in one place for long, unless it is in front of her easel to paint the gorgeous landscapes, figures, and light-filled still lifes that have made her a locally revered artist or in the kitchen to bake, and whatever she produces is simply delicious.

These are a play on the traditional Norman sablé, a plain vanilla butter cookie. With all of the wild hazelnut trees that grow in our part of Normandy, it's no wonder so many of the nuts find their way into the local fare, particularly pastries. This is just one, simple example.

2 cups (280 g) unbleached
all-purpose flour

Generous pinch of fine sea salt

½ teaspoon ground cinnamon,
preferably Vietnamese

8 tablespoons (1 stick/110 g)
unsalted butter, at room
temperature

⅔ cup (130 g) sugar

1 large egg

1 generous tablespoon fresh
lemon juice

¾ cup (125 g) hazelnuts, ground
(¾ cup)

Note: *The dough is very fragile and can easily be over-worked. Rolling it out more than once risks making the cookies tough. To solve the problem, I roll out the dough and cut as many cookies from it as I can, using one of my champagne flutes as a cookie cutter because its delicate size is perfect. I shape the scraps into a roll, as gently as I can so I don't overwork the dough, then either refrigerate or freeze it so it becomes firm. Once the dough is firm, I cut it into 1/4-inch-thick rounds and bake those.*

1. Sift together the flour, the salt, and the cinnamon onto a piece of parchment or wax paper.

2. Place the butter in a large bowl or the bowl of an electric mixer and mix until it is softened and malleable. Slowly incorporate the sugar, mixing until it is combined thoroughly with the butter and the mixture is quite light. Mix in the egg until it is combined thoroughly, then slowly add 1 cup of the flour mixture, mixing well. Then mix in the lemon juice. Add the remaining flour, mixing just until it is combined, then add the ground hazelnuts and mix just until combined. The dough will be quite soft and thick.

3. Refrigerate the dough for 8 hours or overnight to give the ingredients a chance to meld and to harden the dough enough so that it can be rolled out.

4. Preheat the oven to 375°F (190°C). Line two to three baking sheets with parchment paper.

5. Roll out one-fourth of the dough on a lightly floured surface until it is about ¼ inch (.6 cm) thick. Using either a champagne flute or a cookie cutter that measures about 1½ inches (4 cm) across, cut out as many rounds as you can from the dough. Place the rounds on a prepared baking sheet, leaving about ½ inch (1.25 cm) between the cookies. Gently press together the scraps of dough and form them into a roll that measures 1½ inches (1.25 cm) in diameter. Wrap the roll of dough in plastic wrap or parchment and refrigerate it for an hour or two so it will firm up enough to be cut into thin rounds. (The dough will keep very well in the refrigerator, if well wrapped, for at least 1 week. It can also be frozen for up to 3 months at this point.) Repeat with the remaining dough.

6. Bake the cookies in the center of the oven until they are golden—they will darken more at the edges than in the center—about 10 minutes. (For that little log of dough that remains, you can slice it into rounds and bake them as above.) Remove the cookies and let them cool to room temperature on a wire cooling rack. They will keep in an airtight container for about 3 days.

Wenatchee Apple Torte

❧ *Makes 6 to 8 servings*

I was a newspaper reporter in Wenatchee, Washington, home of America's major apple industry. In my stint there I spent a good deal of time working for the food section of the paper, searching out local food stories and recipes. This one came my way from an elderly woman named Viola, and I've been making it ever since. Simple and forthright, the crunch of the nuts, the moisture of the apple, and the fragrance of the coconut guarantee it a ready audience.

⅔ cup (90 g) unbleached all-purpose flour

2 teaspoons baking powder

¼ teaspoon fine sea salt

2 large eggs

1 cup (200 g) vanilla sugar (page 10)

1 teaspoon vanilla extract, preferably from Madagascar vanilla beans

1 medium, tart-sweet apple, such as a Fuji, Gravenstein, or Cox orange pippin, peeled, cored, and diced (1 cup)

1 cup (100 g) walnuts, coarsely chopped

½ cup (45 g) unsweetened shredded coconut

Note: *When whisking in the dry ingredients, take care not to overmix, which can cause toughness by over-developing the gluten in the flour.*

Unsweetened coconut is available at health food and specialty stores.

1. Preheat the oven to 350°F (180°C). Butter and flour a 6 × 10-inch (15 × 25-cm) glass baking dish.

2. Sift the dry ingredients onto a piece of parchment or wax paper.

3. In a medium bowl or the bowl of an electric mixer, whisk the eggs until light and frothy. Whisk in the vanilla sugar and vanilla extract and continue whisking until the mixture is pale yellow. Whisk the dry ingredients into the egg mixture just until combined, then fold in the apples and nuts. Pour the batter into the prepared baking dish, sprinkle the coconut over all, and bake in the center of the oven until the torte is golden, 25 to 30 minutes.

4. Remove the torte from the oven and let cool to room temperature before serving.

Joanne's Pfefferneuse—Spiced Walnut and Almond Cookies

🍀 *Makes 75 to 80 cookies*

I received this recipe from my friend Joanne Kneft, who refers to them as pfefferneuse. They do resemble the hard, pepper-spiced German holiday cookie, but these are softer and more appealing, and they contain no pepper!

Walnuts, almonds, and almond paste give these cookies flavor and moist texture; the addition of dried fruit, spices, and honey makes them very good keeping cookies. While they are Christmasy, they are welcome long after the festive season, perfect for dunking in a cup of strong coffee or a glass of rich white Burgundy.

Note: *These cookies are infinitely better 2 weeks after they are baked, as the spices have settled and gotten acquainted, the honey has reached out to enfold everything, the flavor is mellow and gentle. If you don't have time to bake all the cookies at once, don't be concerned— the dough keeps well, tightly covered and refrigerated, for almost a week.*

- 1¼ pounds (4¼ cups) unbleached all-purpose flour
- 1 tablespoon baking soda
- ½ teaspoon fine sea salt
- 1 tablespoon ground cinnamon
- 1½ teaspoons freshly grated nutmeg
- 1½ teaspoons freshly ground allspice
- 1 teaspoon freshly ground cloves
- Scant 2½ cups (9 oz/260 g) walnuts, minced (about 2 cups)
- Generous 1 cup (120 g) almond flour or finely ground almonds
- 4 tablespoons (½ stick/60 g) unsalted butter, softened

1. Sift together the flour, baking soda, salt, and spices onto a piece of wax paper or parchment. Using your fingers, mix in the minced walnuts and almond flour.

2. In a large bowl or the bowl of an electric mixer, blend the butter, vanilla sugar, and almond paste, mixing until thoroughly combined. Add the egg, mixing well, then add the honey, vanilla extract, and lemon zest and mix until combined. Add the dry ingredients alternately with the milk, beginning and ending with dry ingredients. Stir in the candied orange peel until it is thoroughly incorporated into the dough. The dough will be quite stiff. Cover and refrigerate overnight.

3. Preheat the oven to 325°F (165°C). Line several baking sheets with parchment paper.

4. Remove the dough from the refrigerator. Roll 1 table-spoon of the dough into a ball. Place on a baking sheet. Repeat with the remaining dough, leaving at least 1 inch (2.5 cm) between balls so the dough has room to spread.

5. Bake the cookies in the center of the oven until they are puffed and golden and don't spring back when you touch them, about 17 minutes.

6. Transfer the cookies to cooling racks. When they are completely cool, store them in airtight containers for at least 1 week before eating. Because of the honey in the cookies, which acts as a preservative, and the low fat content, these cookies keep for months in an airtight container. They won't stay around that long, of course . . .

½ cup (100 g) vanilla sugar (page 10)

4 ounces (60 g) almond paste

1 large egg

1 cup (about 8 ounces/250 g) mild honey, such as wildflower or lavender

½ teaspoon vanilla extract

Zest of ½ lemon, minced

¼ cup (60 ml) milk

4 ounces (120 g) candied orange peel, minced

Lemon Madeleines with Pistachios

🍀 *Makes about 36*

Fresh lemon zest and pistachio nuts permeate these elegant little cakes, which make not only for good memories but also for lovely moments of immediate pleasure! I like to serve these either with coffee or as a dessert, warm from the oven.

Note: *One of the tricks to a successful madeleine is to have the pans and the batter cold and the oven quite hot. This way the little cakes will rise in the center, creating the characteristic bump that has become a hallmark of a good madeleine. If you don't have enough madeleine pans to bake all the batter, simply turn out the hot baked madeleines, wipe the pans clean, rebutter them, and use the remaining batter. The batter will keep well in the refrigerator for at least 3 days, so you can easily bake these and serve them warm, on demand.*

- Butter and flour for the madeleine tins
- 1¾ cups (250 g) all-purpose flour
- Pinch of fine sea salt
- Zest of 2 lemons, minced
- 3 tablespoons pistachio nuts, salted and minced
- 4 large eggs
- 1 cup (200 g) vanilla sugar (page 10)
- 6 ounces (1½ sticks/180 g) unsalted butter, melted and cooled to room temperature

1. Butter and generously flour three madeleine pans (each of which makes 12 madeleines). Refrigerate the prepared pans.

2. Sift the flour and salt onto a piece of wax or parchment paper. Add the lemon zest and pistachios and, using your fingers, mix them into the flour mixture.

3. Place the eggs and the vanilla sugar in a large bowl or the bowl of an electric mixer and whisk until very thick and pale yellow. Fold in the flour, then the melted butter so all the ingredients are thoroughly incorporated.

4. Spoon a generous tablespoon of batter into each mold so it is nearly full. Refrigerate the filled madeleine pans and the remaining batter for at least 30 minutes. Alternatively, chill the batter overnight, tightly covered.

5. Heat the oven to 450°F (230°C).

6. Bake the madeleines just until they are puffed and your finger leaves a slight indentation in the top when touched lightly, 7 to 8 minutes. Turn them out immediately from the molds. The madeleines are best when eaten slightly warm or at room temperature the same day they are made.

Lena's Nut Cookies

🌸 *Makes about 56*

My dear friend Lena Sodergren, a tall, gorgeous Swedish woman whom I've known for many years and who is my favorite friend in Louviers, has inherited a love for baking, baked goods, nuts, and a host of other delicious foods from her Swedish culture. These simple butter cookies are a good example and the first recipe she shared with me when she heard I was working on this book. These little gems—and they are little—melt in your mouth and fill it with the most luscious, rich, balanced toasty flavor. Don't be tempted to make the cookies bigger—they are intended to be a one-bite affair, because they are so tender.

Note: *Lena suggests grating the nuts rather than chopping them, which results in a coarsely ground nut that gives off a more intense flavor than a chopped nut. I agree with her, and I grind the nuts for this recipe in a Mouli grater, the kind with a barrel that fits into a handle and is generally used for grating Parmigiano-Reggiano. If you don't have one, just finely chop them by hand.*

13 tablespoons (180 g) unsalted butter, at room temperature

½ cup (100 g) vanilla sugar (page 10)

2¼ cups (300 g) all-purpose flour

¼ teaspoon fine sea salt

⅓ cup (50 g) almonds, lightly toasted and finely ground or chopped

⅓ cup (50 g) hazelnuts, lightly toasted, skinned, and finely ground or chopped

1. Preheat the oven to 350°F (180°C). Line two baking sheets with parchment paper.

2. In a large bowl or the bowl of an electric mixer fit with a paddle, cream the butter with the vanilla sugar until the mixture is soft and pale yellow.

3. In a medium bowl, combine the flour, salt, and nuts, using your fingers to mix them all together. Stir the nut mixture into the creamed butter and sugar and mix just until the dough adheres—it will be quite crumbly.

4. Using a teaspoon of dough, gently form small balls—they won't be perfectly round, but this isn't important—and place them 1½ inches (4 cm) apart on the prepared baking sheets. Using the tines of a fork, gently press on the balls to flatten them.

5. Bake in the center of the oven until the cookies are golden, 10 to 12 minutes. Remove from the oven, transfer to a wire rack, and let cool. These little cookies will keep for 1 week in an airtight container.

Hazelnut Cakes—Financiers

❧ *Makes about twenty-one 1¾ × 3½-inch (4 × 9-cm) financiers*

I include the French name of this well-loved cookie, *financier*, because it is almost mythical among cake and cookie lovers. Named for its shape—the same as a gold brick—this little cake is traditionally made with ground almonds. You'll find this hazelnut version even more delicious than the original, and I based this recipe on one that I helped develop when I was working on the *Food Lover's Guide to Paris* with Patricia Wells.

Note: *If you don't have financier molds, which are rectangular and quite heavy, you may use madeleine molds or cupcake tins. Just be sure to butter them well and be careful about the baking time. The yield, too, is likely to change.*

12 tablespoons (1½ sticks/165 g) unsalted butter, melted and cooled

1½ cups (140 g) hazelnut flour or very finely ground hazelnuts

1⅔ cups (225 g) confectioners' sugar

½ cup (70 g) unbleached all-purpose flour

Pinch of salt

¾ cup egg whites (5 or 6 eggs)

1. Preheat the oven to 450°F (230°C). Using a pastry brush, thoroughly butter about twenty-one individual financier molds using some of the melted butter intended for the financiers. Arrange the molds side by side but not touching on a baking sheet. Place the baking sheet with the molds in the freezer so the butter solidifies and so the financiers unmold easily.

2. In a large bowl, combine the hazelnut flour, confectioners' sugar, all-purpose flour, and salt. Mix to blend. Add the egg whites and mix until thoroughly blended. Add the remaining melted butter and mix until thoroughly blended. The mixture will be fairly thin.

3. Pour or spoon the batter into the molds, filling them almost to the rim. Place the baking sheet in the center of the oven. Bake until the financiers are pale gold and begin to firm up, about 7 minutes. Turn off the oven and leave the financiers to sit in the warm oven for 7 minutes.

4. Remove the financiers from the oven and let them cool in the molds for 10 minutes, then unmold them onto a cooling rack to cool completely. These financiers are best the day they are made.

Coconut, Pistachio, and Chocolate Macaroons

🌿 *Makes about 45 cookies*

I must thank my friend and colleague David Lebovitz for this confection, though I do take credit for the pistachio nuts, which add their incomparable color and flavor to what was already one of the best-ever sweets. These are so simple, so luscious, and so professional looking that you'll be very proud to make and serve them. I sent this recipe to Marion Pruitt, my good friend and colleague and U.S. recipe tester. When she read that the cookies would keep for a week, her response was the following: "You must be kidding! These won't keep for 'about one week'! Made them last night with a yield of forty-three, and half were gone by this morning. There are only two people living here (that I know of)."

Note: *The recipe calls for unsweetened coconut, which is available at health food and specialty stores. If you can find only salted pistachios, simply drop them into boiling water, remove and drain them, let them dry for an hour or so, and proceed with the recipe.*

The dough for these cookies will keep for up to 1 week in the refrigerator.

1. In a large, heavy saucepan over medium-low heat, mix together the egg whites, vanilla sugar, salt, honey, coconut, flour, and pistachios. Stir the mixture frequently until it softens and becomes somewhat runny, then stir it almost constantly, scraping the bottom of the pan, until it dries out and pieces of it begin to turn golden—15 minutes total. Remove the pan from the heat and stir in the vanilla. Transfer the mixture to a piece of parchment paper set on a work surface to cool to room temperature. At this point, you may refrigerate the dough.

- 4 large (120 g) egg whites

- 1¼ cups (250 g) vanilla sugar (page 10)

- ¼ teaspoon fine sea salt

- 1 tablespoon mild honey, such as wildflower or lavender

- 2½ cups (215 g) unsweetened shredded coconut

- ¼ cup (35 g) all-purpose flour

- 3 tablespoons pistachios, lightly toasted and minced

- ½ teaspoon vanilla extract

- 4 ounces (110 g) bittersweet or semisweet chocolate, coarsely chopped

2. Preheat the oven to 350°F (180°C). Line two baking sheets with parchment paper.

3. Using a generous teaspoon of the dough, form small balls that you flatten on one side and bring to a round point on the other so that each little cookie looks like a wide cone. Place the cookie on a prepared baking sheet, leaving about ½ inch (1.25 cm) between cookies, until you have used all the dough. Bake until the cookies are deep golden brown, about 16 minutes. Remove from the oven, transfer to a cooling rack, and let cool completely.

4. While the cookies are baking, melt the chocolate in a double boiler. Line a baking sheet with parchment paper. When the cookies are cool, dip the flat bottoms into the chocolate and swirl it slightly so the chocolate climbs up the side of the cookie just a bit, then set the cookies on the prepared baking sheet. When the chocolate has hardened, either serve the cookies or store them in an airtight container. The cookies will keep for about 1 week.

Rocky Road

David Lebovitz, infinitely creative pastry chef, friend, and co-teacher, made this recipe for my two children the first time he came to visit. They've loved him ever since! And I loved learning how simple it is to make such a great candy, but I prefer to make my own marshmallows. If you lack the time, the courage, the machine, or the ingredients, just buy marshmallows and make this. Your family, your friends, your colleagues—all will fall to their knees with pleasure.

Note: *It is vital, when melting chocolate, not to cover it, as condensation forms on the inside of a cover and will drip into the chocolate and "freeze" it.*

Try any salted nut here that appeals to you, or use a mix of several varieties.

1. Line a baking sheet or pan with parchment paper.

2. To melt the chocolate, place it in the top of a double boiler. Place the double boiler over medium-high heat, bring the water to a boil, reduce the heat to medium-low, and leave the chocolate to melt, uncovered. Remove from the heat and let it cool slightly so it isn't blistering hot.

3. Transfer the chocolate to a large bowl and add the nuts, marshmallows, and cocoa nibs, if using, folding them into the chocolate until they are well mixed.

4. Turn out the mixture onto the prepared baking sheet and spread it out as much as possible. Leave it to

- 1¼ pounds (560 g) semisweet chocolate (52–62%) such as Lindt or Ghirardelli, coarsely chopped
- 1½ cups (210 g) roasted salted almonds (try Marcona almonds, from Spain) or toasted salted peanuts, coarsely chopped
- About 2 cups (100 g) marshmallows, cut into ½-inch pieces
- ½ cup (60 g) roasted cocoa nibs (optional)

cool at room temperature, then cut it into pieces. Serve immediately or store in airtight containers kept in a very cool place. It is not necessary to refrigerate the rocky road, which will keep well for about 10 days.

Peanut and Sesame Brittle

🌸 *Makes about 2½ pounds (1.25 kg)*

Caramel, peanuts, and sesame seeds combine to make this version of an American favorite. I love the crunch of this and its tiny bite of salt, which highlights the toasty nuts and seeds.

Note: *The sesame seeds are added with the baking soda to prevent them from overcooking.*

3 cups (600 g) vanilla sugar (page 10)

1 cup light corn syrup

Heaping ½ teaspoon fine sea salt

2 tablespoons (30 g) unsalted butter, cut into 4 pieces

3 cups (480 g) raw peanuts

¼ cup (35 g) sesame seeds

1 tablespoon baking soda

1. Butter a large (at least 2½-foot/76-cm square) heat-resistant surface such as marble or granite.

2. Mix the vanilla sugar and corn syrup with ½ cup (125 ml) water and the salt in a large, heavy saucepan over medium-high heat. Bring the mixture to a boil and cook, stirring occasionally, until the mixture turns golden and reaches the hard ball stage (about 265°F/130°C) on a candy thermometer, up to 10 minutes.

3. Add the butter and peanuts, stir, and return to a boil. Cook until the mixture reaches the hard crack stage (about 310°F/155°C), another 5 to 10 minutes. Remove from the heat and stir in the sesame seeds and baking soda. The mixture will bubble up, so stir vigorously to calm it down. Let the mixture sit for about 30 seconds to allow it to quit bubbling entirely, then pour it out onto the prepared surface.

4. Immediately spread out the mixture as thin as you can, using a metal or wooden spatula. Don a pair of thick rubber gloves and, as the brittle cools but before it gets hard, begin pulling on it from every direction to stretch it, distribute the peanuts evenly, and give it a shiny gold luster and brittle texture. It should stretch to almost double its original size.

5. When the brittle is cooled and hard, break it into pieces. It will keep for 2 weeks in an airtight container stored in a cool place.

Pistachio Ice Cream

The beauty of this ice cream is its rich and mellow pistachio flavor and color, which is a natural deep ivory rather than the artificially bright green we're used to seeing in pistachio ice cream. Creamy and satisfying, this ice cream is delicious right after it is made, when still in the "soft serve" state, or several hours later, when it has had a chance to harden a bit.

Note: *I ask you to strain the custard before you turn it in the ice cream maker so that the crushed nuts don't stop the ice cream maker from working. This nugget of wisdom comes from experience—the paddles on my very efficient little ice cream maker simply won't turn beyond any chunks or bumps, and I assume your machine is the same. I suggest you stir the nuts back into the ice cream so they can add not only their flavor but also their texture. In all the tests of this ice cream that I have done, it's the version with the nuts that wins the flavor prize!*

4 ounces (110 g) raw shelled pistachio nuts

Tiny pinch of salt

1¼ cups (250 g) sugar

1 quart (1 liter) half-and-half

6 large egg yolks

1. Crush the pistachios to a paste using a mortar and pestle with the salt and ¼ cup (50 g) of the sugar.

2. Place the pistachio mixture in a heavy saucepan with the half-and-half and whisk them together. Place the saucepan over medium heat and scald the half-and-half. Remove from the heat, cover, and let infuse for 1 hour.

3. Set a large bowl near the burner where you are making the custard.

4. In a large bowl, whisk together the egg yolks and the remaining 1 cup (200 g) of sugar until they are thick and pale yellow. Slowly whisk the warm half-and-half and pistachios into the egg yolk and sugar mixture, then transfer that mixture to a heavy saucepan over medium heat. Stirring constantly in a figure-eight pattern, cook the custard until it thickens and allows the utensil you are using to glide easily across the bottom of the pan. If this takes longer than 10 minutes, increase the heat slightly, but be sure not to boil the mixture or it will curdle.

5. When the custard is thick, immediately pour it into the large bowl. Let the custard cool to room temperature. Refrigerate until it is chilled.

6. To make the ice cream, first strain the custard so the crushed nuts don't inhibit the action of the ice cream maker, then follow the ice cream manufacturer's instructions for turning ice cream. If you want the texture of the crushed nuts in the ice cream, simply stir them back into the ice cream once it is solid.

Nougat Glacé

This is certainly a bit of heaven on a plate—and so easy to make. I got the recipe from my friend Eloise Perret, a passionate home cook who is undaunted by any recipe she finds. This is one of the best she has ever sent my way. Filled with crisp, caramelized almonds and pine nuts, studded with delicious dried fruit, and perfumed with orange flower water, it is both ethereally light and delicate and stunningly satisfying. The first time I served this to my wine-tasting group, I thought they would riot over the slices left in the pan. So I say this serves ten to twelve, but it really depends on the voracious-ness of the appetites present!

Note: *Traditionally, nougat glacé is served with a raspberry sauce, which is delightful. I prefer to serve this perfect nougat on its own, however, with just a few fresh berries sprinkled around it. If you don't have fresh berries, use frozen that you've let thaw just slightly. And if you don't have either, serve this on its own. I call for dried apricots here. I get them unsul-fured, from Turkey, and they can be a bit hard, so I cover them with boiling water for about 2 minutes, drain and pat them dry, then coarsely chop them. You can find orange flower water at thespicehouse.com*

1. Oil a baking sheet or heatproof work surface. Line two 9×5×3-inch (23×13×8-cm) loaf pans with plastic wrap, leaving plenty hanging over the edges.

2. Place the sugar and ½ cup (125 ml) water in a medium, heavy saucepan over medium heat. Whisk them together. The mixture will first simmer, then as it thickens it will begin to bubble stickily. You don't need to hover over it until it begins to turn golden. At that point, stay close, as it

FOR THE NOUGATINE:

1 cup (200 g) sugar

1½ cups (230 g) almonds, lightly toasted

¼ cup (40 g) pine nuts

FOR THE LIAISON:

2 cups (500 ml) heavy non-ultrapasteurized cream

2 teaspoons orange flower water

3 tablespoons mild honey (if you can find lavender honey, use it!)

3 large egg whites

Pinch of fine sea salt

4 dried figs, diced

½ cup (95 g) dried apricots, rehydrated and patted dry if necessary, diced

can go from golden to black very quickly, and what you are looking for is a deep golden color. The minute it is deep golden, stir in the almonds and pine nuts; the mixture will tend to clump, but keep stirring so the caramel coats all the nuts. Turn out the mixture onto the oiled baking sheet or surface, spread it out as best you can, then let it cool. When it is thoroughly cool, slip it into a double plastic bag and crush it by hitting it with a rolling pin. What you are looking for is unevenness—some clumps of whole caramelized almonds and some dust.

3. In a large bowl, whisk the cream into stiff peaks, then whisk in the orange flower water and reserve, chilled.

4. Heat the honey until it is nearly at the boiling point and remove from the heat. In the bowl of an electric mixer, whisk the egg whites with the salt until they are white and making soft points. Pour the hot honey into the egg whites as they are whisked, until the egg whites are glossy and stiff. Be careful not to pour the hot honey right onto the whisk, or it will spatter.

5. To assemble the nougat, fold the crushed and caramelized nougatine into the whipped cream along with the dried fruits, then fold the egg whites into the fruit and nut mixture. Turn out half the mixture into each of the prepared loaf pans. Gently fold the edges of the plastic wrap over the nougat and place the pans in the freezer to freeze for at least 8 hours, preferably overnight. This will keep in the freezer for up to 1 week, tightly wrapped.

6. To serve, unwrap the nougat and turn it out onto either a cutting board or a serving plate and slice it into serving-sized pieces. Garnish it with the berries, if using. Serve immediately, while it is still thoroughly chilled.

2 to 3 cups (9 to 14 ounces) fresh berries, preferably raspberries, for garnish (optional)

Jacqueline's Walnut Cake

🌸 *Makes 10 servings*

Jacqueline is the aunt of a very good friend of mine, Eloise Perret, and this cake is a bastion of Jacqueline's baking prowess. What I love the best of the many cakes I've sampled from Jacqueline's kitchen is their simplicity and very French minimalist quality, which takes advantage of the most perfect-quality ingredients.

This cake, which has bread crumbs in it instead of flour, is one of her best. The framework is walnuts—from Normandy, where Jacqueline lives in the town of Lisieux—and each mouthful is like a sweet, light hymn to their delicate, nutty flavor.

Note: *The walnuts aren't toasted before being baked in the cake because sometimes it is wonderful to taste their pure, buttery flavor. However, if toastiness is what you prefer, lightly toast the walnuts before you add them to the cake. Whisk the egg whites just until they form soft peaks, not a bit further or the cake will be dry.*

- 1²/₃ cups (280 g) walnuts
- 1 cup plus 2 tablespoons (225 g) sugar
- 6 large eggs, separated
- 2 teaspoons vanilla extract
- 1 tablespoon fresh bread crumbs
- Generous pinch of salt

1. Line a 9½-inch (24-cm) springform pan with parchment paper, then butter the parchment paper and the sides of the pan. Preheat the oven to 350°F (175°C).

2. Process the walnuts and 2 tablespoons of the sugar in a food processor until the walnuts are very finely ground. Be careful not to overprocess as the nuts can become oily.

3. In a large bowl or the bowl of an electric mixer, whisk together the egg yolks, vanilla extract, and all but 2 tablespoons of the remaining sugar until they are thick and pale yellow. Fold in the ground walnuts and bread crumbs.

4. In a large bowl or the bowl of an electric mixer, whisk the egg whites with the salt until they are very foamy and just beginning to form soft peaks. Whisk in the reserved 2 tablespoons of sugar and continue whisking until the mixture is glossy and forms soft peaks.

5. Fold the egg whites into the walnut and egg yolk mixture until thoroughly combined. Turn the mixture into the prepared pan and bake until the cake is golden and puffed and your finger leaves a slight indentation on the top when you press it gently, about 35 minutes.

6. Remove the cake from the oven and let it cool on a wire rack for 30 minutes. Remove the cake from the pan and let it cool completely. Transfer it to a serving platter and serve.

Golden Pound Cake Crowned with Nuts

❦ *Makes 10 servings*

There is a saying in France when something tastes so good you cannot believe it, that it is like "Jesus in velvet pants." This cake is that. I was inspired to make this after buying a cake similar to this in a lovely little bakery in the Montmartre neighborhood of Paris. It was as if the cake reached out and grabbed me, it was so lovely. I tasted it, then made it just a few days later because it had to go in this book.

It is really a simple pound cake all dressed up. The nuts, glistening from their wash of apricot glaze, make it regal, fit for a grand occasion or a very special cup of tea!

Note: *The leavening in this pound cake is simply egg whites beaten with a bit of sugar. Don't be tempted to add baking powder, which tends to dry out a cake of this sort. The egg whites are all it needs.*

1. Preheat the oven to 350°F (175°C). Butter and flour a 9-inch (23-cm) springform pan, then line the bottom with parchment paper and butter the parchment paper.

2. Sift the flour with a generous pinch of salt onto a piece of parchment paper.

3. In the bowl of a mixer or in another large bowl, mix together the butter and all but 2 tablespoons of the vanilla sugar until they are pale yellow and light. Add the egg yolks, one at a time, mixing just until they are combined. Add the vanilla extract, then slowly mix in the flour just until it is combined.

4. In a separate bowl, whisk the egg whites with a pinch of salt. When they are light and foamy and beginning to

1½ cups (210 g) unbleached all-purpose flour

Fine sea salt

14 tablespoons (1¾ sticks/210 g) unsalted butter, at room temperature

1 cup (200 g) vanilla sugar (page 10)

4 large eggs, separated, at room temperature

2 teaspoons vanilla extract

1½ cups (about 200 g) mixed nuts, such as cashews, walnuts, and almonds, lightly toasted

½ cup (125 ml) apricot jam

turn white, slowly add the remaining 2 tablespoons of sugar and whisk just until they form soft peaks.

5. Fold one-fourth of the egg whites into the batter, then gently fold in the remaining egg whites just until the mixture is homogenous. Do not overfold, or the egg whites will lose their volume.

6. Turn the batter into the prepared pan. Evenly sprinkle the top of the cake with the nuts and bake the cake in the center of the oven until it springs back when touched but isn't dry, about 35 minutes.

7. Strain the apricot jam into a small, heavy saucepan over low heat. Stir in 1 teaspoon water and cook just until the glaze is liquid. Remove from the heat.

8. Remove the cake from the oven and place it on a wire rack. Immediately brush the glaze generously over the nuts, then let the cake cool for at least 20 minutes before removing the edges of the pan. When the cake is cooled completely, remove it from the bottom of the cake pan.

Lena's Poppy Seed Cake

🍀 *Makes one 9-inch (23-cm) round cake; 8 to 10 servings*

Score another home run for the Swedes in this gorgeous cake, which is the Swedish version of a brownie. Like a brownie, it stays chewy in the center. The traditional way to serve it is buried in whipped cream. In my home we just eat it plain. With its seed-popping texture, it quickly becomes addictive.

Note: *Poppy seeds are used to "flour" the pan to prevent the cake from sticking. They create a crisp outer layer on the cake, and their nutty "pop" is lusciously, intriguingly delicious. I think you'll find yourself "flouring" many a cake pan this way!*

- ½ cup (60 g) poppy seeds
- 1½ cups (210 g) unbleached all-purpose flour
- 1 teaspoon baking powder
- Generous pinch of salt
- 2 large eggs
- 1½ cups (300 g) vanilla sugar (page 10)
- 2 tablespoons diced candied orange peel
- Zest of 1 lemon, preferably organic, minced
- ¼ cup (60 ml) fresh lemon juice
- 12 tablespoons (6 ounces/180 g) unsalted butter, melted

1. Preheat the oven to 350°F (175°C). Generously butter a 9-inch (23-cm) pan. Sprinkle ¼ cup of the poppy seeds over the bottom and sides of the pan. Leave any excess poppy seeds on the bottom of the pan.

2. Sift together the dry ingredients onto a piece of wax or parchment paper.

3. Whisk together the eggs and vanilla sugar in a large bowl until they are pale yellow and lightly foamy, then whisk in the candied orange peel, lemon zest, remaining ¼ cup of poppy seeds, the lemon juice, and the melted butter. Fold in the dry ingredients and turn the batter into the prepared pan.

4. Bake in the center of the oven until the cake is puffed and golden and the surface is shiny and somewhat crackly, about 45 minutes. Remove from the oven and place on a cooling rack. After 20 minutes, turn out the cake onto the rack and cool to room temperature before serving.

Fiona's Yogurt Cake

🌿 *Makes about 8 servings*

Fiona, when she was nine years old, came home from a day of activities at the local community center, her eyes shining. "Mom, we made a cake today, and I copied down the recipe for you," she said. I looked at it, and déjà vu whooshed through me: it was the yogurt cake recipe I'd discovered in one of my son Joe's classes when he was about her age. Fiona's was different, but equally simple to make, and delicious!

Fiona has been instrumental in the creation of this book, as she has dutifully sampled, cheerfully offered suggestions ("What about a recipe for homemade Nutella, Mom? *That* would have nuts in it"), and keenly hoped that I would use one of her recipes as part of this collection. In fact, I've included two, and this is one of them!

⅓ cup (50 g) almonds, lightly toasted

1½ cups (210 g) unbleached all-purpose flour

¾ teaspoon baking powder

Pinch of fine sea salt

¼ cup (22 g) unsweetened shredded coconut

3 large eggs

1 cup (200 g) sugar

½ cup (125 ml) whole-milk yogurt

1 teaspoon vanilla extract

8 tablespoons (1 stick/125 g) unsalted butter, melted and cooled

Note: *This simple cake improves with age. If you make it the night before you plan to serve it, you'll see that the flavors become richer, more mellow.*

Unsweetened coconut can be found at health food and specialty stores.

1. Place the almonds in a food processor and process until they are finely ground. Be careful not to over-process so they don't turn oily.

2. Heavily butter a 9½-inch (24-cm) round cake pan. Place the ground almonds in the pan and shake the pan so that the almonds evenly cover the bottom. Preheat the oven to 375°F (190°C).

3. Sift together the dry ingredients onto a piece of wax or parchment paper. Add the coconut and mix together using your fingers.

4. In a large bowl, whisk together the eggs and sugar until they are light and pale yellow. Sprinkle the dry ingredients over the eggs and sugar, whisking to incorporate them as you do. Fold in the yogurt and vanilla, then the melted butter.

5. Pour the batter into the prepared cake pan. Bake the cake in the center of the oven until the cake is slightly mounded and your finger leaves a very slight impression when you touch the top of it, 35 to 40 minutes.

6. Remove the cake from the oven and let it cool in the pan. To serve, place a serving plate on top of the cake pan and flip the pan so that the cake emerges from it with the almonds on top. Serve immediately.

Crumbly Almond Cake—Sbrisolona

🍀 *Makes about 10 servings*

This cake, which is really a giant cookie, will send you to heaven on a sweet, nutty little ride. The recipe comes from Patricia Wells, my dear friend and cohort, who loves the same kinds of things I do, including Paris, food, and nutty, not-too-sweet creations like this one.

Patricia got this recipe from a woman named Rosetta Gasparini, part of the kitchen team at the Villa Minora, owned by the Allegrini wine family. Patricia was near Verona when she met them, thanks to the offices of a mutual friend of ours, Italian gastronome Rolando Beremendi. Rolando is responsible for putting, among other people, the Rustichella pasta company on the culinary map, and he was indispensable to me when I worked on *Italian Farmhouse Cookbook.* His magic doesn't cease, as he is continually putting good food, good people, and good experiences together.

Patricia returned from a trip to Italy so excited about this recipe that it was in my mailbox within hours of her return, after she'd had time to unpack her bags and test it. When you make it, you will understand why!

2 cups (300 g) whole unblanched almonds, lightly toasted

2¼ cups (300 g) unbleached all-purpose flour

¾ cup plus 2 tablespoons (140 g) polenta, instant polenta, or fine cornmeal

½ teaspoon fine sea salt

9 ounces (2¼ sticks/260 g) unsalted butter, melted and cooled

Note: *This isn't a cake, and it isn't a cookie; it is both. Follow the directions exactly, then serve this lovely large creation whole and have guests break off pieces the size that suits them. This can be either a mid-morning accompaniment to coffee, or an after-meal dessert with a glass of sweet Vin Santo.*

As for the number of people it will serve, well, there are three people who live in my house, and with a couple of hungry passersby we ate it all up.

Note that you may use either fine cornmeal or instant polenta in this recipe.

¾ cup (150 g) vanilla sugar (page
    10)

1 large egg

1. Preheat the oven to 350°F (175°C).

2. Set aside 10 almonds for garnish and place the rest in a food processor. Coarsely chop them—they will be uneven in size, which is fine.

3. In a medium bowl, combine the chopped almonds, flour, polenta, and salt. Toss to blend. Set aside.

4. In a large bowl, combine the melted butter, vanilla sugar, and egg and whisk to blend. Add the dry ingredients and stir to combine until the mixture is homogenous. The texture should be like that of cookie dough.

5. Rub the dough between your hands and let it drop onto the baking sheet so that it covers the sheet without any spaces showing—this creates a gorgeous, uneven surface. Scatter the reserved whole almonds on top of the dough.

6. Place in the center of the oven and bake until deep golden and crisp, 20 to 30 minutes. Let cool before serving. Don't be tempted to cut this with a knife—break off pieces of it with your fingers.

Walnut Coffee Tourte with Coffee Frosting

🍀 *Makes one 9-inch (23-cm) round cake; 10 to 12 servings*

I owe this recipe to Linda Dallas, an artist who lives in North Carolina and was one of my cooking students. She not only taught me the value of the catchall southern phrase "Bless her heart" but shared this recipe with me, after she'd entered it in a baking contest, where it won first prize. When you taste it, you will see why! It is mouthwateringly cozy yet very dressed up, the kind of cake Mom might have made when she was entertaining her friends for an afternoon bridge game and wanted to both satisfy and impress.

Despite the relative intensity of the coffee, a flavor sometimes too strong for a child's palate, my kids, and every child I've fed this to, love this cake. They are attracted by its fancy style—three thin layers, tempting icing that gracefully garnishes the layers and the top, and golden walnut halves that finish it off. But they return for more because of its moistness and flavor.

This is a cake that will easily serve twelve. It also keeps well. I keep it on a plate at room temperature, with a bowl over it, for a week or more.

FOR THE CAKE:

1⅔ cups (225 g) unbleached all-purpose flour

2 teaspoons baking powder

Heaping ¼ teaspoon fine sea salt

¾ pound (3 sticks/1½ cups/360 g) unsalted butter, at room temperature

1⅔ cups (330 g) vanilla sugar (page 10)

Note: *This cake is best if left to sit for several hours or overnight before serving. If you do refrigerate this cake, it will emerge somewhat drier than when it went in.*

1. Preheat the oven to 350°F (175°C). Butter and flour three 9-inch (23-cm) round cake pans. Line the pans with parchment paper and butter and flour the parchment paper as well.

2. Sift together the dry ingredients onto a piece of parchment paper.

6 large eggs

¼ cup (25 g) walnuts, lightly
  toasted and minced

½ cup (125 ml) very strong
  brewed coffee

½ teaspoon vanilla extract

FOR THE FROSTING:

16 tablespoons (8 ounces/250 g)
  unsalted butter, softened

1⅔ cup (200 g) confectioners'
  sugar

⅓ cup (80 ml) strong brewed
  coffee, chilled

1 teaspoon vanilla extract

⅛ to ¼ teaspoon fine sea salt

FOR THE GARNISH:

¼ cup (25 g) walnut halves,
  lightly toasted

3. In a medium bowl or the bowl of an electric mixer, whisk the butter and the sugar until they are pale yellow and light. Whisk in the eggs one at a time, whisking each time until the egg is thoroughly incorporated. Using a large spatula or wooden spoon, fold in the dry ingredients, then the walnuts. Finally, fold in the coffee and vanilla extract.

4. Divide the batter equally among the three pans, smoothing out the batter. The pans will be less than half full, which is fine. Bake the cakes on the center rack of the oven until they are slightly puffed and your finger leaves a slight indentation on the top of the cake when you press it lightly, about 25 minutes. Transfer the cakes to cooling racks and turn them out of the pans after they have cooled for 10 minutes.

5. To make the frosting, in a medium bowl or the bowl of an electric mixer, whisk together the butter and confectioners' sugar until they are pale yellow and light. Add the coffee and vanilla extract and whisk until the mixture is smooth, then whisk in the salt to taste.

6. When the cakes are cooled thoroughly, place one on a serving platter. Top it with one-third of the frosting, then set the second cake on top and frost the top of it. Repeat with the remaining cake. Decorate with the toasted walnut halves and let sit for an hour or more before serving.

The Basics

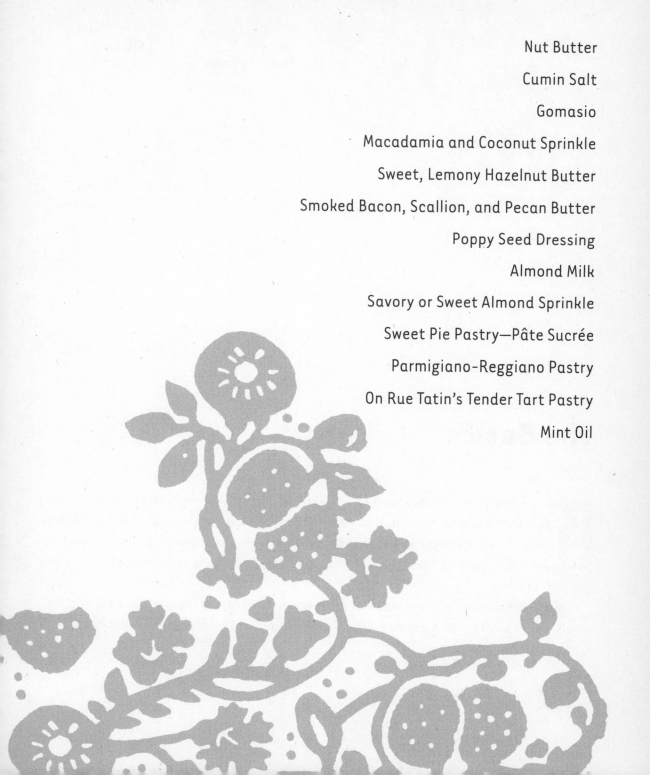

Nut Butter

Cumin Salt

Gomasio

Macadamia and Coconut Sprinkle

Sweet, Lemony Hazelnut Butter

Smoked Bacon, Scallion, and Pecan Butter

Poppy Seed Dressing

Almond Milk

Savory or Sweet Almond Sprinkle

Sweet Pie Pastry—Pâte Sucrée

Parmigiano-Reggiano Pastry

On Rue Tatin's Tender Tart Pastry

Mint Oil

The Basics

Basic recipes are the backbone of a cookbook, for without them many other recipes are often nothing more than empty shells. The basics can also be little jewels that shine on their own, to be made and kept on hand for those impromptu moments when you want a meal to appear as though it had been a long time in the planning when in fact it came together in haste.

Consider these basics a cooking class that arms you with the framework of many great meals. Let's say you've just steamed some vegetables and a piece of fish. Shower the fish with

Macadamia and Coconut Sprinkle and toss the vegetables with Smoked Bacon, Scallion, and Pecan Butter. Voilà, a quick and well-seasoned meal is yours. You can liven up your breakfast with hazelnut butter—or any homemade nut butter—and flavor your next sauce with mint oil. With a handful of basics in your pantry, life and your meals will take on a new dimension.

Nut Butter

🌿 *Makes 1 cup (250 ml) nut butter*

Homemade nut butters are so fresh, so richly flavored and textured, that when you begin to make your own, you may never buy them again.

Use these nut butters to thicken soups and sauces, to slather on bread or toast, to put in a sandwich. They can be used anywhere you use peanut butter.

2 cups (300 g) raw nuts

Fine sea salt

Note: *It takes almost 15 minutes for a food processor to turn warm, toasted nuts into fine, delicious nut butter. Don't be tempted to add oil at any stage of the process, as nuts contain all the oil they need to make a beautiful butter.*

1. Preheat the oven to 350°F (175°C).

2. Place the nuts in a baking pan and bake in the oven until they are golden and smell toasty, 7 to 10 minutes. Remove from the oven and transfer the nuts directly to a food processor. Process the nuts until they turn to butter, which will take approximately 15 minutes. The nuts will go through several stages before they begin to turn to a puree and become oily. First they'll be coarsely chopped, then more finely chopped, then minced, then they'll take on a rough, dusty aspect. At this point you may think you need to add oil—don't! Let the processor continue to run. The nuts will become finer and begin to turn oily.

Don't turn off the food processor until you have a fine puree, a beautiful nut butter.

3. Transfer the nut butter to a container. Don't seal the container until the nut butter has completely cooled. Stored in an airtight glass jar, in the refrigerator, it will keep for about 2 weeks.

Cumin Salt

I like to have seasoning mixtures like this on hand to dress up a meal. Cumin salt is a favorite because the intense flavor seems to enhance just about everything. I sprinkle it over freshly sliced cucumbers dressed with lemon oil, avocados drizzled with pistachio oil, fish fillets, eggplant, a potato gratin straight from the oven, or fresh chard sauteéd until tender.

¼ cup very fresh and fragrant cumin seeds

2 tablespoons plus 2 teaspoons fleur de sel

Note: *This mixture doesn't last forever, which is why I make it in small quantities. This way it is always fresh and sprightly with flavor.*

I prefer to grind the cumin and the salt using a mortar and pestle, because it produces a mixture that is nicely combined but still has much of its delicate crunch. If you don't have a mortar and pestle, do this in a coffee grinder used only for spices, but be gentle about it—you don't want fine dust but a full-textured mixture.

1. Place the cumin seeds in a small, heavy skillet over low heat and toast them until they turn golden and begin to emit a fragrant aroma, 2 to 3 minutes. Remove them from the heat and transfer them to a mortar or a spice or coffee grinder. Add the salt and grind the spices together until they are ground uniformly but coarsely. The mixture should be very "sprinkleable."

2. Store the cumin salt in an airtight container in your spice drawer or another dark, cool spot. It will keep for up to 3 months.

Gomasio

Gomasio is a Japanese seasoning that goes in everything from soup to rice. Used heartily in the macrobiotic diet, it is a tasty addition to anyone's diet. Simple to make, it keeps for a long while, thanks to the nature of the sesame seed, which is reluctant to oxidize and turn rancid.

Note: *My gomasio is quite salty—you can adjust according to your palate. Prepare for rave reviews for this seasoning! A special mortar with a ridged interior, called a* suribachi, *is made just for gomasio, and it works like a dream. If you don't have one, use either a regular mortar and pestle or a food processor.*

- 1 cup (140 g) sesame seeds
- 2 tablespoons fine sea salt

1. Place the sesame seeds in a wok or other heavy pan over very low heat. If your flame won't turn to very low, put a heat diffuser on it to reduce the heat. Toast the sesame seeds, stirring occasionally, until you begin to smell their toastiness and hear them pop. Stir so they all get their chance at contact with the pan (and even toasting), then turn them out onto a wood work surface or into a large bowl. Cool.

2. When the sesame seeds are cool, grind them using a (suribachi) mortar and pestle or in a food processor, not too fine. You don't want dust; you simply want to crack up the sesame seeds a bit so you can sprinkle the gomasio. Stir in the salt until thoroughly combined with the sesame seeds. Store in an airtight container, preferably one that is opaque. It doesn't need to be refrigerated.

Macadamia and Coconut Sprinkle

🍀 *Makes about 1⅓ cups (180 g)*

As I've worked on this book over the last couple of years, I have loved having all sorts of nut preparations in my pantry, ready to enliven everything from breakfast cereal to pasta. This particular combination is a lovely addition to both sweet and savory dishes. I prefer it atop the fish in the Marinated Fish with Sesame and Macadamias (page 115), but try it on breakfast cereal or hot oatmeal, atop pancakes or folded into their batter, on rice that is either sweet or savory, or by the spoonful when no one is looking.

¾ cup (100 g) macadamia nuts, lightly toasted and coarsely chopped

⅓ cup (30 g) unsweetened coconut

Note: *The recipe calls for unsweetened coconut, which is essential. Presweetened coconut won't work. Unsweetened coconut is available at health food and specialty stores.*

1. Place the macadamia nuts and coconut in a nonstick skillet over medium heat and cook, shaking the pan often and stirring, until the coconut turns a nice, dusty golden brown, about 8 minutes. The nuts will also be perfectly toasted by then.

2. Remove from the heat and let cool thoroughly. Either use immediately or store in an airtight container out of the light. In the refrigerator, it will keep for at least 2 weeks.

Sweet, Lemony Hazelnut Butter

🌸 *Makes 1 cup (250 ml)*

This spread is like peanut butter gone *way* uptown. I enjoy it most on freshly toasted bread in the morning, but you can also use it on crackers, between cookies (à la Oreo), or in a cake icing.

Note: *This will keep well for 1 month in the refrigerator in an airtight container.*

1. Place the sugar and lemon zest in a food processor and process until completely combined. The sugar will be just slightly damp from the oil in the zest.

2. In a food processor, process the lemon sugar and the hazelnuts until the nuts are finely ground. Add the butter and lemon juice and continue processing until all of the ingredients are thoroughly mixed. Transfer the mixture to a serving bowl or a glass jar. If not using immediately, refrigerate for up to 1 month, remembering to remove the hazelnut butter from the refrigerator at least 15 minutes before serving. Otherwise it can be difficult to spread.

1 cup (200 g) sugar

Zest of 2 lemons, preferably organic

2/3 cup (100 g) hazelnuts, lightly toasted and skinned

1/4 pound (1 stick/110 g) unsalted butter, at room temperature

1/2 teaspoon fresh lemon juice

Smoked Bacon, Scallion, and Pecan Butter

🌰 *Makes 1½ cups (325 ml)*

This gem is from Sue Raasch, who uses her own pecans—either native or papershells—for everything from soup to nuts. I love this particular recipe, which is so simple to put together and so great to have on hand. Use it on freshly steamed green beans, cauliflower, broccoli, or even turnips or Brussels sprouts. Try it on rice, grains, or grilled steak or fish, or tucked under the skin of poultry that you intend to roast. It enhances nearly everything!

½ pound (225 g) slab bacon, without skin, cut into ¼-inch (.6-cm) pieces

3 scallions or spring onions, trimmed of half their green stalk and diced (¼ cup)

¼ cup (30 g) pecan pieces, lightly toasted

12 tablespoons (1½ sticks/180 g) unsalted butter, at room temperature

Fine sea salt and freshly ground black pepper

Note: *You may use "pecan pieces," which are broken pieces of pecan that have all the flavor of a good, whole pecan. They are often more reasonably priced than whole pecans. Whatever form you buy, make sure they are fresh and do not look brown or oily, and check the "sell by" date, too.*

If you cannot find slab bacon, buy thick-sliced bacon. This butter will keep in the refrigerator for three to four days. Alternatively, you can freeze it.

1. In a medium, heavy skillet over medium heat, fry the bacon until browned on all sides, 8 to 10 minutes. Remove from the pan and let cool. Discard any fat given up by the bacon.

2. Place the bacon with the scallions and pecans into a food processor and pulse until combined. Add the butter and continue to process until all the ingredients are well blended. Season with salt and pepper to taste.

3. To store any excess, shape the butter into a log, wrap in parchment paper or plastic wrap, and refrigerate for up to 1 week or freeze—preferably in portion sizes, so you can remove just one portion at a time—for up to 3 months.

Poppy Seed Dressing

🌿 *Makes about ⅓ cup (80 ml)*

This is a wonderful sauce for vegetables, for fish, even for meat straight off the grill. I also like to serve it as a dipping sauce for fresh bread.

1 tablespoon fresh lemon juice

Zest of ½ lemon, minced

Fine sea salt

2 tablespoons poppy seeds

¼ cup (60 ml) extra virgin olive oil

1. Place the lemon juice in a small bowl along with the zest, a pinch of salt, and the poppy seeds. Slowly whisk in the olive oil until the dressing is emulsified. Taste for seasoning. This will keep in an airtight glass container in the refrigerator for about 4 days. Just remember to take it out about 30 minutes before you plan to use it, as it's best served at room temperature.

Almond Milk

Almond milk is so delicate, so pure, so lightly creamy that it almost defies description. I make it primarily so that I can make blancmange (page 180), though almond milk is good in coffee, it's delicous poured over granola, and it's delectable poured over fresh fruit or added to vegetable soup. You'll find many uses for it.

You can purchase almond milk, but it won't have the fresh flavor this does. And this is so simple to make it seems a shame not to do so!

Note: *Plan ahead, because the almonds need to soak overnight before being ground with water to make the milk. Once you've extracted the milk from the almonds, you will still have a great deal of richly flavored almond pulp. Turn this into the savory or sweet sprinkles that I suggest on page 234.*

1½ cups (225 g) raw almonds with skins

1. Place the almonds in a medium bowl, cover them with water, and refrigerate overnight.

2. Prepare a fine-mesh sieve by lining it with a double layer of cheesecloth and setting it over a bowl.

3. Drain the almonds and place them in a blender or food processor with 1½ cups (375 ml) filtered water. Process until the almonds are quite finely chopped. Add another 1½ cups (375 ml) filtered water, process, then pour the mixture into the prepared sieve. Let the almond milk drain from the almonds, then, to encourage it, wrap the almond pulp in the cheesecloth and press firmly on it to remove as much milk as possible.

Savory or Sweet Almond Sprinkle

❧ *Makes about 1½ cups (240 g)*

After making Almond Milk (preceding recipe), you will have a great deal of almond pulp left over, and it will still be filled with almond flavor and nutrition. So, with my increasing appreciation for having flavored nut mixtures on hand for sprinkling on everything, I decided to transform that almond pulp into something I would love to use on everything from fresh toast to soup, salad, or pasta. This will keep for about 1 month, in an airtight container in a cool, dry spot.

FOR THE SAVORY VERSION:

1½ cups (240 g) almond pulp from making Almond Milk (page 233)

1½ teaspoons fleur de sel or fine sea salt

1 tablespoon Hungarian paprika, preferably hot, though you can use medium or mild

2 teaspoons ground ginger

1 teaspoon ground star anise

FOR THE SWEET VERSION:

1½ cups (240 g) almond pulp from making Almond Milk (page 233)

3 tablespoons vanilla sugar (page 10)

2 teaspoons ground cinnamon, preferably Vietnamese

½ teaspoon ground allspice

Note: *The almond pulp will be very wet after the milk is squeezed from it, so once you've mixed in the spices you need to dry it thoroughly. It loses a lot of volume as it dries.*

1. Line a jelly-roll pan with parchment paper. Preheat the oven to 210°F (100°C).

2. Place the almond pulp in a medium mixing bowl and add the spices for the savory version or the sugar and sweet spices for the sweet version. Mix thoroughly. The pulp will be quite damp, so spread it in an even layer on the prepared pan and place the pan in the oven to dry and toast, which could take as long as 2 hours. Check on it from time to time, and as it begins to turn golden, check on it more frequently. Remove from the oven and let it cool thoroughly before storing it in an airtight container.

Sweet Pie Pastry—Pâte Sucrée

🍀 *Makes enough pastry for a 10½-inch (27-cm) tart*

This is a wonderfully easy all-purpose pastry for fruit and other tarts. It goes together quickly and easily—do not lose heart at the point where it looks like a mass of crumbles. Follow the recipe and you'll get a beautiful pastry.

Note: *You may make this in the food processor, but it isn't as good and tender, and the ingredients don't go together quite as well as when it is made by hand. When you put the ingredients in the well, don't leave the sugar touching the egg yolks and then walk away or become distracted before continuing with the recipe. Sugar will "cook" raw egg yolks, making little hard pieces of egg yolk. When you begin this recipe, finish it straight through for the best results.*

- 1¾ cups (230 g) unbleached all-purpose flour
- ½ teaspoon fine sea salt
- ½ cup (100 g) vanilla sugar (page 10)
- 4 large egg yolks
- 8 tablespoons (1 stick) unsalted butter, at room temperature but still firm

1. Sift the flour onto a work surface and make a large well in the center. Place the salt, vanilla sugar, and egg yolks in the well and mix them with your fingers. Pound on the butter to soften it slightly, add it to the well, and quickly combine it with the other ingredients, using the fingertips of one hand, until partly blended. Gradually work in the flour with the fingertips of both hands, pulling the flour from the side toward the butter mixture in the center, until large crumbs form. Continue blending the pastry by cutting it into pieces using a dough scraper. When the dough is smooth, gather it into a ball, then continue to work it by pushing it away from you and against the work surface with the heel of your hand and gathering it up with the dough scraper until it is pliable and thoroughly combined. Press the dough into a flat round and let it sit in a cool place for at least 30 minutes. Roll it out as specified in the recipe.

Parmigiano-Reggiano Pastry

❧ *Makes enough pastry for a one-crust tart or about thirty 4 to 5 × ½-inch (10 to 13 × 1.25-cm) sticks*

This pastry is a simple inspiration, a recipe I am so happy to have in my repertoire. I make it often, using it either as a base for a savory mixture (see the Grilled Vegetable Tarts with Pumpkin Seeds, page 68) or as a simple appetizer after rolling it out, cutting it into thin strips, and baking it to a crisp golden turn (see Parmigiano-Reggiano Seed Sticks, page 40).

1 cup (145 g) unbleached all-purpose flour

Pinch of fine sea salt

4 ounces (120 g) Parmigiano-Reggiano cheese, finely grated

7 tablespoons (100 g) unsalted butter, chilled, cut into 14 pieces

5 to 6 tablespoons (75–90 ml) ice water

Note: *This is very easy to make—just pay attention to letting the pastry sit out at room temperature so the gluten in the flour can relax, making it easy to roll out.*

1. Place the flour, salt, and cheese in a food processor and pulse once to mix. Add the butter and process until the mixture resembles coarse meal, pulsing five to eight times. Add 5 tablespoons (75 ml) ice water and pulse just until the pastry begins to hold together and is quite damp. Add another tablespoon of water if the pastry seems dry.

2. Transfer the pastry from the food processor to your work surface and form it into a flat round. Let it rest on the work surface, covered with a tea towel or a bowl, for at least 30 minutes and as long as 1 hour.

On Rue Tatin's Tender Tart Pastry

🍀 *Makes enough pastry for one 10½-inch (26-cm) to 12½-inch (31-cm) tart*

I call this On Rue Tatin pastry because I teach students how to make it in every single class I offer. The reason? Because it is perfect. Easy and quick to make, always delicious, crisp, and buttery, it can embrace anything, whether it be sweet or savory.

Note: *Pay careful attention and have both the butter and the water as cold as possible before adding them to the other ingredients. If you are working in a very hot environment, refrigerate the flour before making this.*

1½ cups (210 g) unbleached all-purpose flour

¼ teaspoon sea salt

12 tablespoons (1½ sticks/180 g) unsalted butter, chilled and cut into 12 pieces

5 to 6 tablespoons (75–90 ml) ice water

1. Place the flour and salt in a food processor and pulse once to mix. Add the butter and process until the mixture resembles coarse meal. Add 5 tablespoons (75 ml) ice water and pulse just until the pastry begins to hold together. If the pastry seem dry and dusty, add another tablespoon of water.

2. Transfer the pastry from the food processor to your work surface and form it into a flat round. Let it rest on the work surface, covered with a bowl, for at least 30 minutes. The pastry can sit for several hours at room temperature, as long as the room isn't warmer than 68°F (20°C). The pastry is ready to use as desired.

Mint Oil

Flavored oils are delicious additions to many dishes. Mint oil is commonly used as a seasoning or a condiment in Turkish dishes, and I'll never forget the first time I enjoyed it, drizzled over Potatoes with Yogurt and Pistachios (page 160). I was in Gazientep enjoying a meal prepared by Fatih Babican, an extraordinary chef who is devoted to his native Anatolian cuisine. I was surprised he used dried mint in the oil, but he pointed out how much more intense its flavor is when freshly dried, and on tasting this oil I had to agree with him. Try using this on hummus, on steamed fish, on roasted chicken right from the oven, or even as a dip for sesame bread.

⅓ cup (80 ml) extra virgin olive oil

1 tablespoon dried peppermint leaves

Note: *Make sure not to boil the olive oil when infusing it, as that will denature its flavor. Heat it gently, just enough so that the heat of the oil encourages the flavor from the dried peppermint, which must be very, very fresh and pungent. The oil is at the perfect temperature when you can dip the back of your index finger into it and feel the heat but not get burned. Mint oil will keep for about 3 days, refrigerated. Remove it from the refrigerator about 20 minutes before you plan to use it, so it can liquefy.*

1. Place the olive oil and the mint in a small, heavy pan, whisk them together and place over very low heat, and heat the oil just enough so the temperature increases enough to feel hot when you touch it with the skin on the back of one of your fingers. Do not let it boil. Keep the oil at this temperature for about 10 minutes, then remove from the heat and reserve.

Index